D1123877

THE
GREAT
MOTION
MISSION

A SURPRISING STORY OF
PHYSICS IN EVERYDAY LIFE

BY CORA LEE
ILLUSTRATED BY STEVE ROLSTON

annick press
toronto + new york + vancouver

Text © 2009 Cora Lee
Illustrations © 2009 Steve Rolston

For Jaime (quark-and-
leprechaun comic),
Peter (key gluon in the
nuclear family),
and Dora (alter-
entangled ego)

Annick Press Ltd.

Edited by Pam Robertson
Copyedited by Geri Rowlatt
Proofread by Elizabeth Salomons
Cover and interior design by Matt Heximer & Susan Lepard at 10four design group
Cover and interior illustrations by Steve Rolston

We acknowledge the support of the Canada Council for the Arts, the Ontario Arts Council,
and the Government of Canada through the Book Publishing Industry Development
Program (BPIDP) for our publishing activities.

**ONTARIO ARTS COUNCIL
CONSEIL DES ARTS DE L'ONTARIO**

Cataloguing in Publication

Lee, Cora
   The great motion mission : a surprising story of physics in everyday life / by Cora Lee ;
illustrations by Steve Rolston.

Includes bibliographical references and index.
ISBN 978-1-55451-184-6 (pbk.) ISBN 978-1-55451-185-3 (bound)

   1. Physics—Juvenile literature. I. Rolston, Steve II. Title.

QC25.L44 2009   j530   C2009-901160-3

Published in the U.S.A. by
Annick Press (U.S.) Ltd.

Distributed in Canada by
Firefly Books Ltd.
66 Leek Crescent
Richmond Hill, ON
L4B 1H1

Distributed in the U.S.A. by
Firefly Books (U.S.) Inc.
P.O. Box 1338
Ellicott Station
Buffalo, NY 14205

Printed and bound in China

Visit our website at www.annickpress.com

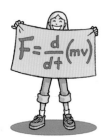

What does the formula on the cover of this book mean?

$$F = \frac{d}{dt}(mv)$$

F stands for force
d/dt stands for "derivative of" and expresses a rate of change
m stands for mass
v stands for velocity

WHAT YOU'LL FIND INSIDE

Chapter 1   page 1
Introduction

Chapter 2   page 7
Physics in Action: Aerodynamics, Momentum,
and Winning the Game
Featured Physicist: Sir Isaac Newton

Chapter 3   page 23
Physics and Sight: Photons, the Electromagnetic
Spectrum, and the Art of Seeing
Featured Physicist: Albert Einstein

Chapter 4   page 37
Physics and Sound: Longitudinal Waves,
Harmonics, and Making Music
Featured Physicist: Marie Curie

Chapter 5   page 51
Physics in and Around Us: Thermodynamics,
Atoms, and Worlds Big and Small
Featured Physicists: Erwin Schrödinger,
Werner Karl Heisenberg, and Paul Adrien Maurice Dirac

Chapter 6   page 67
Physics in Motion: Gravity, Acceleration, and
Fun at the Fair
Featured Physicists: Stephen Hawking and
Richard Feynman

Chapter 7   page 81
Physics and Our Electronic Existence:
Conductivity and Our Favorite Devices

Glossary   92

Further Reading   106

Index   109

Photo Credits   113

About the
Author and Illustrator   114

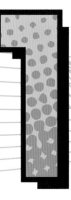

Don't get me wrong. Like any sane, freedom-loving kid, I start itching for summer vacation the day school starts— but now that summer's come, it's shaping up to be kind of dull.

Why? Well, my main mission in life is to have fun. And right now, it seems like a conspiracy's operating against that. Threat No. 1: Sam's not around. It's not like I don't have other friends, but he's right next door. Sure, I could've gone with him on exchange, but can you see *me* studying at math camp all summer? I had other plans.

Or so I thought. Then along comes Threat No. 2: the city's shutting down the summer fair for the first time ever, and probably for good. The university wants to build a new physics research center on the fairgrounds. It's practically a done deal—all they need is the mayor's signature. They're holding a physics conference on the site next week to celebrate and show off the site to the scientists. So instead of kids swarming the coaster and scarfing down corn dogs, physicists will be parking where the rides are now and scoping out the blueprints inside—when they're not listening to each other's lectures, of course. Oh, or teaching summer physics camp—

physics?

What's physics?

...It's discovering the sources of push-and-pull forces, the ups and downs of energy. It's figuring out what stuff is made of and what holds it together, from deep inside the atom to far-out stars and galaxies. Physics is making sense of how things are connected in our space and time—maybe even beyond. In short, it's the exploration of everything.

basically, free classes they're offering kids to take the place of the amusement park rides. Right. Don't everybody rush to register! Real geniuses there at the university.

After the conference, construction begins. Apparently the whole thing's a big honor for our little town and everybody's thrilled, according to the news. Everybody, huh? Guess they forgot to ask me.

They must've missed Liam, too. Liam's my uncle, and he's lived in our basement forever. He's all right, but I don't exactly advertise the fact that we're related. He writes for the local paper, a cool job—in the right hands. But in his newspaper columns, he keeps calling me "Jeremy, the little boy upstairs with the dark curls." I mean, come on. Maybe he's forgotten the growth spurt that made me so much taller than him. I can't stand the way he talks, either. His voice is way too big for his size, just like his swelled head. He's always bragging about something. Anyway, we do have one thing in common. We both wish this conference—the XIV Symposium on the Universality of Physics—and building project would just disappear. He's supposed to write up the conference for the newspaper and, well, he's definitely got a phobia when it comes to physics.

"Physics! In high school, I skipped it when I could and slept through it when I couldn't." Liam actually whimpered when he said this. He recovered quickly enough, but you could still hear the panic under all the complaining. "All that research I'll have to do is a waste of my brain space and talent. When will I ever need physics again? It's an insult, that's what it is. I can think of a dozen assignments better suited to a journalist of my caliber."

I felt for him, I really did, but I had problems of my own: namely, Threat No. 3, the final reason why this will be the worst summer ever. I said Sam was on exchange, right? So this girl Audrey's staying with his family. Sam's parents told my parents, who asked me—more like told me—to make sure I include Audrey in all my plans, so she's not lonely so far from home. I said sure, no big deal, but I wasn't expecting a visitor from Mars!

JEREMY WRESTLES WITH THE WEIRD STUFF...

Hello...? Is anybody out there? Audrey says serious scientists are involved in the Search for Extraterrestrial Intelligence (SETI), and so is she. She's signed on with the SETI@home project, which borrows her home computer whenever she's not using it. While Audrey's off with friends, SETI@home throws up a screensaver and gets busy analyzing strange patterns of radio signals from space. Over 3.8 million people from 226 countries are chipping in computer time—feeding SETI's massive need for number-crunching power. Each computer executes 2.4 to 3.8 trillion mathematical operations on just one chunk of the endless stream of data picked up by radio telescopes and receivers worldwide. Physicists figure that if what they're seeing aren't radio bursts from pulsars (collapsed stars that emit regular signals as they rotate) or interference and hoaxes from Earth, then, hey, maybe an advanced alien civilization's trying to contact us!

She's only from the other side of the country, but where's an intergalactic translator when you need one? In Scrabble the other day, she racked up points using words my teachers wouldn't know (go ahead, ask yours): I mean, who knew qubit, quark, and branes were legit? To me, cosmic means amazing. To her, it describes whole other galaxies.

qubits, quarks, branes, gluons, and muons…top-secret code words, or signs of physicists having some fun to lighten things up? It's a tough slog, figuring out the secrets of the universe…speaking of which, what do those weird words mean anyway? Read on!

She looks normal enough. On the tiny side, and pale. Straight, blonde hair. Two serious gray eyes. One nose, one mouth; two arms, two legs. She wears the same stuff other girls wear but is more into the kind of comics and movies I like. But come on…I mean, get this: she can't wait till the physics conference starts. What's that got to do with us, says stupid me. Aren't you going to do their camps for kids? she asks, with this look of surprise. My mother—always lurking at the worst possible moment—immediately signed me up. Why didn't I keep my mouth shut?

Two seconds later, Audrey had left, my mother was back inside, and I was left sitting there, stunned by science, on my own front steps. It didn't help when Liam came whistling up our walk. "You're awfully cheerful," I said in a sour voice, "for someone who's spending the summer studying physics."

"Oh, but I won't be," said Liam with a grin. "I've got a plan."

Liam looked around cautiously before continuing. "A protest will do it. I'll just convince everyone they need the fair more than they need physics."

This sounded promising. "How?"

"With my powers of persuasion, I can do anything," boasted Liam. "It occurred to me: these scientists—they have no right to bring in their 'cutting-edge' ideas to 'improve' our lives." If Liam's sneer weren't so funny, it'd be scary. "All we know is what they tell us: the good stuff, the promises. Who knows what risks—and there's always a risk with technology—they're hiding? Who are they to force our children to suffer the studying? Somebody's got to protect our innocent citizenry from the pitfalls of progress," he continued. "And who better than me? *I* live here, *I* know the hearts and minds of the people, *I* have the ability. I'll need some help from the kiddy contingent, of course—that's where you come in."

Let the "kiddy" comment go, I told myself...he could be my way out of a sad situation. "Depends on what you need me to do. And it's got to be undercover, okay?" No way was I letting Audrey find out.

"Check the morning paper," Liam said, opening the door and heading in. "And remember, I'll be at the baseball diamond tomorrow to interview your team about the big tournament. Just follow my lead."

I didn't even get a chance to pick up the paper the next day before Audrey was over. "Hey, take it easy on the door," I said.

"Look at this!" she said, jabbing the headline: "Physics over Fun: No Fair—In More Ways than One." I read it, or tried to, which wasn't easy with Audrey whipping the page around and stomping every which way. *...as well-intentioned parents blinded by the tinsel-wrapped promises of technology rush to register their kids in the Symposium's physics camps, this reporter begs them to reconsider... The UN Convention on the Rights of the Child includes the right to play...Too much sedentary study time leads to childhood stress, obesity...end of the fair and permanent closure of the amusement park...bored youth sick of studying, fearful of a physics-filled future...can only mean trouble ahead for this community.* Liam ended his article by challenging everyone to come to the public meeting at the fairgrounds that night to tell the mayor what they thought.

Way to go, Liam! I took the smile off my face as Audrey wheeled around. "What if he drives the conference away?" she railed. "What if the mayor changes his mind about the new research center?"

"What if he does?" I shrugged and picked up my glove and bat. "Who needs it?"

Audrey glared at me. "Your life wouldn't be the same without physics," she said. "Nobody's would. I'm going to prove that to Liam, and you're helping me."

"Me?" I yelped. "No way! And anyway, I've got to get to practice. Liam's waiting for me afterward, too."

"Perfect," said Audrey. "I'll come with you."

Great. Showing up with Audrey wasn't, I'm sure, what Liam had in mind. Telling Audrey why I couldn't help her—because I agreed with Liam and would do anything to avoid physics camp—was, well, suicidal. I was going to have to play both sides, and carefully: from now on, I was undercover *and* a double agent.

Liam was at the baseball diamond, as promised. After practice, he took a few photos, but he didn't ask many questions about the tournament. In fact, he kind of rushed through the interview. Slowing down finally, he looked hard at every player in turn. Still sweating and dusty, the guys sitting on the bench squirmed. Poor Lucas took a step back and fell into the bag of base-balls. Personally, I felt a laugh coming. Was I the only one who thought Liam was overdoing it?

At last, Liam spoke. "So. You're the underdogs going in. What will it take to win?"

"I dunno," said Angus finally. "Lots of practice, I guess."

Practice? More like luck, maybe a miracle. I still don't know how we got this far.

"When will you have time?" Liam asked, innocently. "Your parents tell me you're all registered in those fascinating physics classes this summer."

Howls of outrage and dismay greeted this reminder. Poor guys. I knew how it felt—with Audrey, the reminders came daily. Liam raised his voice over the noise. "That's what I want to hear," he said.

"I like how you're willing to practice hard and make sacrifices to win. So tell you what: meet me at the fairgrounds at five p.m., before the meeting about the physics building tonight."

The guys were still grumbling, so Liam jumped onto the end of the bench. "If you kids band together, we can protest!" He had their attention now. "You'll have your extra practice time, AND the summer fair!" His face turned red with effort as he punched the air. "Whatever it takes to win, we'll do it!"

"Then you might want to learn some physics!" Audrey said as she stepped down from the bleachers where she'd been listening in.

"How's sitting in class supposed to help anything?" asked Lucas, our pitcher, whapping a ball hard into his glove.

H ATOM   O ATOM H_2O MOLECULE

time out!

A few basics will get you in the game. Only about a hundred millionth of a centimeter wide (about four billionths of an inch), an atom is a tight package of protons and neutrons, with electrons staking out the surrounding space. Any of these bits we can also call particles, and they move nonstop. Atoms come in 112 types, called elements (think hydrogen or gold) and are the smallest recognizable part of any element. When atoms mix, match, and stick, you get molecules: two hydrogen atoms attached to an oxygen atom is a water molecule. What are atoms and molecules good for? Just building ordinary matter, which is *only* about everything you see in this universe! Five states of matter exist: solid (like wood), liquid (like water), gas (like oxygen), plasma (a hot, gassy mess of electrons and electron-less atoms, like the stuff in neon signs), and Bose-Einstein (BE) condensate (an ultra-dense blob formed by elements like rubidium at super-cold temperatures).

"Show me your best pitch," she challenged.

Lucas stood undecided for a minute before walking over to the pitcher's mound and throwing a ball to Audrey at home plate. Sure, he sounded tough, but truth was, he only had one pitch—which made him, well, kind of predictable.

"That's all you've got?" said Audrey. "You need to know a lot more about aerodynamics."

"Aerodynamics?" Liam made sure we all heard him. "Sounds difficult. Like most physics," he emphasized.

Audrey ignored Liam and said, "Aerodynamics just involves looking at how air and other gases flow and affect solid things moving through them. Air's full of oxygen, nitrogen, and other gas molecules, so a flying ball has to push through a lot to get where it's going…"

"It's not exactly a brick wall," hooted Liam. "Air's easy to get through!"

"You think so? It fights back; you feel it when you run or bike," argued Audrey. "Air has viscosity—air molecules 'stick' to each other and to any surface sliding past. This makes it especially tough for small, slow objects to get through."

"I can't see how you could call air sticky," I protested. "And a ball's not that small, either."

"And," pointed out Lucas, "my pitch isn't *that* slow."

"The viscosity of air is pretty low," agreed Audrey. "Alone, it won't slow a baseball anywhere near as much as a dust speck. But your pitch was definitely slow. What happens is that the air molecules closest to the ball's surface stick to it and pull along their neighbors, too. You end up with a boundary layer, a layer of air that tries to wrap around the ball."

"What do you mean, *tries to?*" I frowned, trying to see this.

"Before it can make it all the way to the other side of the ball," Audrey explained, "the boundary layer starts peeling off. When it peels off, it forms a wide wake—an area with fewer air molecules spread out in choppy whirls—behind the ball and that leads to drag.

Drag means lower pressure, or less pushing power. With high pressure in front forcing it back, and not much pressure behind to stop it, the ball slows down."

SLOW-MOVING BALL, LARGE WAKE

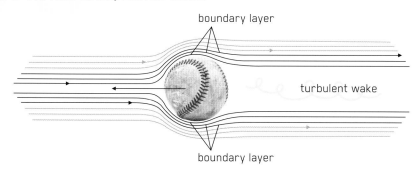

boundary layer

turbulent wake

boundary layer

"I guess you want to reduce this drag, then," Lucas said slowly. "But how?"

"You want a small wake," replied Audrey, "which you get with a ball going faster than 50 miles an hour—80 kilometers an hour if you're into metric—but your pitch was nowhere near that fast. That's when air inside the boundary layer gets turbulent—rough enough to sweep the air farther around the ball—so the boundary layer 'unwraps' later, and you end up with a smaller wake."

FAST-MOVING BALL, SMALL WAKE

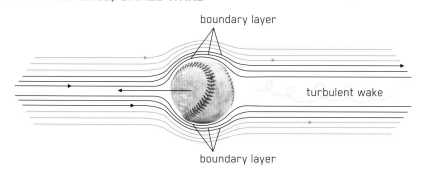

boundary layer

turbulent wake

boundary layer

Audrey watched Lucas rubbing the stitches on the ball in his fingers, thinking this through. "Ball design helps," she said. "Those stitches stir up boundary air. Same with golf-ball dimples and fuzzy tennis balls."

"Cool. I always wondered about those stitches." Lucas, all the guys in fact, were staring at the seams.

This was too much. "Okay, okay," I said. "Throw fast—is that it?"

I yelped, ducking as Audrey whipped a ball at me. It veered away at the last minute.

"Throw fast, and spin it," she said. "Spinning gets you lift forces—which gets a ball swerving away from its expected path. It's great for fooling batters into swinging at the wrong time or place."

"And tricking innocent kids into diving at the ground," I muttered.

aerodynamic forces

rotation

Audrey searched for a stick and scratched a diagram in the dirt.

"Say for a curveball, you spin a ball to the left. On the ball's right side, air in the boundary layer hits passing air head-on and peels off sooner than the part on the left, where it spins with the passing air. This shifts the wake so the ball gets pushed left, and the air right."

"Curveballs don't just curve sideways," I said. "They go down, too."

"Real curveballs are released from above the shoulder so they spin at a tilt," replied Audrey. "The lift forces push at a tilt, too: sideways and down."

"Can you get it swerving any other way?" Lucas asked.

"Just change the direction of the spin," said Audrey. "The only way it won't go is up—even though the backspin on a fastball makes it look like it does. It'll drop less than the batter expects, but even in the major leagues, where baseballs reach 90 miles per hour—that's 145 kilometers per hour—and spin 1,600 times a minute, it's impossible to actually lift it."

Tossing the stick aside, Audrey reached into the bag of baseballs on the ground. The team watched in silence as one after the other, she threw a fastball, curveball, slider, and screwball.

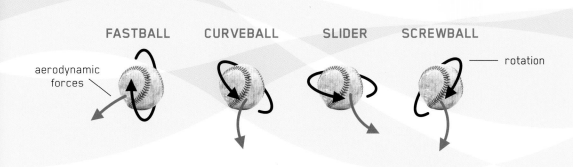

FASTBALL   CURVEBALL   SLIDER   SCREWBALL

aerodynamic forces

rotation

"Same thing in tennis, then…" I said slowly, "when I put topspin on my stroke to drop the ball. And soccer. And golf…" From there, my imagination took off. I was winning game after game in every sport when Liam's loud "ahem" reminded me: focus on the mission.

Lucas tried out his new pitches. Somebody nudged me as I watched. "Hey Jer, do you think physics can help me?"

"She's probably making it up," I said. "I'll bet she's just on a team at home with a good coach." So I lied. Liam gave me a thumbs-up that luckily nobody saw. The guilt will stick with me for months, but whatever it takes…

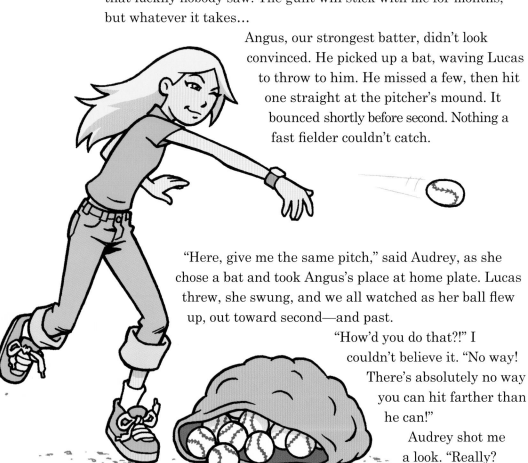

Angus, our strongest batter, didn't look convinced. He picked up a bat, waving Lucas to throw to him. He missed a few, then hit one straight at the pitcher's mound. It bounced shortly before second. Nothing a fast fielder couldn't catch.

"Here, give me the same pitch," said Audrey, as she chose a bat and took Angus's place at home plate. Lucas threw, she swung, and we all watched as her ball flew up, out toward second—and past.

"How'd you do that?!" I couldn't believe it. "No way! There's absolutely no way you can hit farther than he can!"

Audrey shot me a look. "Really? Why?"

"Well, he's...you're..." I looked for help that wasn't coming.

"In one way, you're right," said Audrey, shocking me. "To get distance, you need the ball to leave the bat fast. Lucas's pitch to me had lots of momentum—that's what its mass and speed gave it. What I did was change its momentum, enough to turn it around and speed it up."

massive — a big deal, literally.
The total amount of matter that makes something is its mass. But all matter is made of atoms—and you wouldn't want to count those! An easier way to measure mass is to weigh it.

"All you did was whack it hard," I said.

Audrey rolled her eyes. "Anything that moves has momentum. That 'whack' transferred the momentum from my bat to the ball. There's a physics law that says momentum is conserved in collisions—in other words, the total momentum before and after the collision doesn't change. But it can move. So in the collision, the bat slowed down because its momentum shifted to speeding up the ball."

"Okay, so the bat's got to have lots of momentum," I said, "but you still have to supply muscle somewhere."

Audrey was getting annoyed, I could tell. "Muscle isn't everything!" she exclaimed. "I knew that to get more momentum, the best thing would be to swing a heavy bat really fast. But that's pretty tough to do. A big bat is good, but a fast one is better. So I went for a lighter bat. Most major leaguers use light bats, too."

Angus tried again, this time with the same bat Audrey used. "It still didn't go as far as yours."

"Everyone's perfect bat weight is different," said Audrey. "And it's not only about who hits hardest. Mine stayed in the air longer."

crack! An out-of-the-park home run!

Every bat has a place that's just right for hitting: the sweet spot. Connect there, and all the energy from your swing goes into sending the ball soaring. Connect anywhere else, and you lose energy. Some goes into vibrating the bat, some into jerking the handle—and the ball? It gets what little is left.

"What can you do about that?" Angus argued in defense. "Isn't that gravity?"

"Sooner or later, every ball hits the ground, unless it's caught. But remember how mine went up before curving down?"

"Hey, I know. Like shooting baskets. Aim up like this." I raised my arm diagonally, at a 45-degree angle from the ground.

"That's close." Audrey looked a little surprised. Was I good, or what? What can I say... just a little something I learned from Sam last year.

"But," she continued, "because of drag, the best angle for distance in baseball is really about 35 degrees. Any more than that and the ball pops up. It'd get a long time in the air, but not much distance from home plate.

"Your hit," Audrey said to Angus, "started pretty level and close to the ground. A short drop doesn't leave much time for distance."

"Cool. So for a home run, I should switch to a bat I can swing really fast and hit the ball at a middle-ish upward angle. I can handle that," said Angus.

Liam looked a little alarmed. He cleared his throat and said loudly, "I used to play baseball myself, almost made it to the pros, you know. If it weren't for that unfortunate elbow injury…"

News to me. Who was he kidding?

Audrey guarantees more homers on a ball diamond where humidity (that's the percentage of water in the air), temperature, and altitude are all high. Makes sense. High on top of a mountain, air is 3 percent thinner for every 300 meters (about 1,000 feet) up—so it's smooth sailing for the ball, none of this shoving air aside. Heat spreads air molecules out, too. And where it's humid, light, easy-to-blow-past water (H_2O) molecules replace some of the heavier gas molecules, like oxygen (O_2) and nitrogen (N_2), which are normally in air. Great! All I need is a stadium in the middle of a tropical mountaintop rain forest!

"In my, uh, professional opinion," Liam continued, "you don't need physics. Just practice. But…," he said, switching his attention to Jaime and her friends, who had just arrived on their bikes, "if the team wants to spend all their time studying physics, well, I'm sure other kids have better things to do."

"Like me," said Jaime. "I'm riding every chance I get this summer. Forget physics." Wow. I couldn't ask for better timing. Jaime would never let physics interfere with her sports.

"Forget physics, and you'll slow right down," said Audrey, with a sharp look at Jaime, perched on her racing bike. "Those dropped handlebars get your head down and close-fitting clothes streamline you for a more aerodynamic shape. Plus, when you're drafting right behind another bike, you're riding inside its wake, where the turbulence and low pressure pull you forward. In the Tour de France, cyclists drafting in packs use 40 percent less energy than cyclists who don't."

Sir Isaac Newton
(1642–1727)

When an apple falls…you get bruised fruit. Unless you're Isaac Newton. Then you discover gravity. The 23-year-old was just lounging in the family orchard when it struck him (the idea, not the apple): an apple falls to the ground because the earth attracts it, and the same force traps planets in their orbits around the sun! From here, there was no stopping him: the idea led first to his law of universal gravitation, and ultimately to his three laws of motion that rule how everything in the universe moves.

Newton's brain was in nonstop overdrive. He proved that sunlight split into a rainbow of colors, he worked on developing telescopes, and—since the existing math wasn't up to snuff—he invented a form of calculus to solve problems in his planet studies. There's no doubt he was a brilliant mathematician, astronomer, and physicist. Rumor says, however, that he was also secretive, paranoid, and a little strange. He refused to publish his amazing discoveries unless pushed, and he feuded bitterly with other scientists. When he died, one of his deepest secrets was outed: Newton was also an alchemist, trying to turn other metals to gold and mixing up potions in search of immortality.

Jaime shrugged. "I'm not into racing. Biking's just a good break from the hockey rink. That's where I'd love help, but whoever heard of aerodynamic hockey pads? Anyway, hockey's already the fastest game on Earth."

"A lot of that's power and technique, sure, but the NHL *does* have aerodynamically designed uniforms now," said Audrey. "Two other things help fight friction. Skate blades are sharpened so that only a small part contacts the ice. And the ice surface itself isn't really solid or liquid. It's liquid-like—the molecules in this top layer move differently, so it's not hard like the ice below it, but not flowing like tap water either. Without this layer to make ice slippery, friction would make skating more like scraping on concrete."

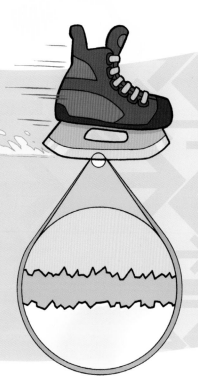

friction —it's that slide-stopping, anti-slip force you get when two touching surfaces move past each other. Its source? Zoom in close: under super-high magnification, even the smoothest objects show up rough, with thousands of jagged teeth that can lock two surfaces like Lego. Fighting friction isn't impossible, though: friction is strongest between rough surfaces that are squeezed tight and standing still—so lighten that load, slick up those surfaces, and start sliding.

Jaime didn't look very convinced, so Audrey tried again. "Hockey depends on other physics, too…"

"I know!" volunteered Angus. "Body checking! Collisions! Just like a bat and ball!"

"We're not allowed to body check in girls' hockey," said Jaime. At Angus's look of disgust, she added, "But who needs to? My stick handling's great, *and* I have a wicked slap shot."

"Slap shots," said Audrey, "are a perfect example of hockey physics. You power up by transferring your weight from back leg to front, then to your stick as you hit the ice."

"The puck, you mean," said Liam with a sneer.

"No, I mean the ice—to bend the stick," said Audrey. "Bending it like a bow loads it up with extra energy. Releasing it off the ice snaps the stick blade at the puck and fires it forward. There's a transfer of momentum from your rotating body to the puck."

"I was half right," said Angus to Jaime. "Collisions and momentum again, see?" He turned to Audrey. "I know spinning the puck off the end of the stick blade is supposed to help your aim, but how?"

"A fast-spinning puck won't wobble," said Audrey. "As soon as it tilts, it'll right itself to keep the angular momentum it gets from spinning."

"Aren't you forgetting a little something called 'ability'?" asked Liam. "Talent scouts don't check for physics degrees."

"Of course ability counts!" protested Audrey. "But physics can't hurt."

"Sheesh—might as well get the team combing the outfield for four-leaf clovers," grumbled Liam. He checked his watch and addressed the team again. "I've got other stories to cover today. So are you with me? Or has the little professor brainwashed you, like she's done with her new puppet?"

I glanced at Audrey and Jaime, busy going over the fine points of physics and the hockey stop. If she couldn't hear Liam, Audrey wouldn't hear me. "So what about it, guys? Let's protest at tonight's meeting."

"I dunno...the distance on that hit...those pitches..."

"We could win this year..."

Were these guys serious? Disgusted, Liam said, "Let's go, Jeremy—the art gallery next."

We snuck away while Audrey was still talking, but it
was no good. She spotted us before we got past the playground next to the baseball diamond, and caught up.
She said nothing, though, the whole two blocks to the gallery. Liam,
on the other hand, went on and on about ball players and their
superstitions.

Inside the foyer, Audrey couldn't hold back and started in on
Liam again. The gallery was one of those dark, stuffy old buildings,
and the foyer, it was the kind that made every whisper seem a
thousand times louder. All the people who kept giving us dirty
looks, I don't blame them one bit. But what could I do? Audrey and
Liam didn't seem to notice. So I just stood, smiling desperately,
between them, wishing I could beam myself out of there.

Liam broke off their argument when he caught the security
guard's eye. "Come on, I have an interview to do," he said.

"What? We're going up with you?" I asked. Art galleries aren't
exactly high on my list of favorite places to visit.

"Yes, I need to take photos of their latest acquisition," said Liam.

"Whoopee," I said. I didn't move.

"Oh come on, one of the exhibits is on comics and cartoons. Not
what I'd call art, but you might like it," said Liam. "And you might
find some kids to talk to."

I got the hint, and Audrey and I followed Liam to the elevator,
where he punched the up button. We got out two levels up, and

Teleportation isn't a science-fiction fantasy anymore! Okay, so it's not quite beaming off *Star Trek*'s *Enterprise* or apparating à la *Harry Potter*. It only works with particles—and the particles don't teleport, just the information describing them. One way of teleporting uses a spooky physics idea: quantum entanglement. Quantum is the physics word for really small; entanglement is the weird way particles can jumble together so that changing one instantly changes the other. So using quantum entanglement, information from an original particle passes through one half of an entangled pair to its faraway partner. Another way of teleporting uses ultra-cold atoms (remember BE condensates from Chapter 2?) to shift data from original atoms into a laser beam and out again to recreate the atoms somewhere else. Sadly, we won't be teleporting people anytime soon. Audrey says moving that much matter (10^{28} atoms) would be really complicated—not to mention lethal. Bummer.

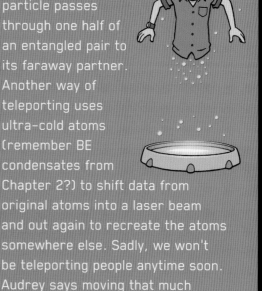

Liam led us down a softly lit hallway. Frowning at Audrey, he said, "Maybe you'll learn something here, too—about a smart bunch of people who don't need physics. Artists and physicists are like different species, see." He swept his arm out over the paintings lining the walls. "All this? Made from 100-percent pure, creative juices. It's as far as you get from dead technical physics. At completely opposite ends of the spectrum."

Audrey pounced on that last word. "A spectrum—the electromagnetic spectrum—is exactly what they have in common!"

She had more to say, I'm sure, but loud, angry voices saved us. At a gallery? Even Liam had toned it down when we exited the elevator.

"What's going on?" Liam asked the guard.

"An unfortunate situation," said the guard, checking Liam's press badge. "Then again, could be a big story for you. You'll have to wait to talk to the curator; he's got a mess to sort out. Looks like the new painting they want could be fake!"

Fake? Now this was interesting.

"Why don't you walk around, take a look at the exhibits," suggested the guard. "He should be available soon."

Liam surveyed the scene. A group of obviously upset people surrounded two stressed-looking men near a painting at the far end of the room—getting through was a definite no-go. Liam sagged against the wall with a sigh. "Why not. Can't do much about this story until those board members are through yelling at the curator."

I started banging the back of my head on the wall. "Save yourself the pain…we can go to the cartoon exhibit," said Liam.

We made our way to that part of the gallery, but the break gave Audrey the chance to start in on that spectrum business again. "As I was saying, artists and physicists have one huge thing in common: the electromagnetic spectrum. Part of it, at least."

"Artists? Whatever you need to know...just ask me," said a voice behind us. Great. I'd forgotten the other reason I avoided the art gallery: this was Oscar's turf. During the summer, he practically lived here, showing off to anyone who'd listen.

"I'm talking about light," said Audrey to Oscar. "None of this artwork exists without visible light—which is radiation in the visible part of the electromagnetic spectrum."

that stuff

you've been calling light your whole life—it's really electromagnetic radiation (EMR), a pair of electric and magnetic fields that wrap around at right angles and endlessly recreate each other in a high-speed race across space. Electro and magnetic, see? And there's more to EMR than meets the eye: visible light is just a small slice of the spectrum. The rest? EMR comes in all sizes, from ultra petite to extra large—or, scientifically speaking, from short, high-energy wavelengths to long, low-energy ones. First up in the spectrum are waves measuring 1 billionth of a meter (about 3 billionths of a foot) or less: cell-zapping gamma rays and x-rays that pierce through muscle and tissue. Then come the ultraviolet rays that sizzle your skin; visible light in rainbow colors; infrared waves with just enough energy to warm you and guide heat-seeking missiles; microwaves—useful for studying the universe and popping corn—and finally, television, cell-phone, and radio waves, measuring in massively at up to a few thousand meters (thousands of feet) long.

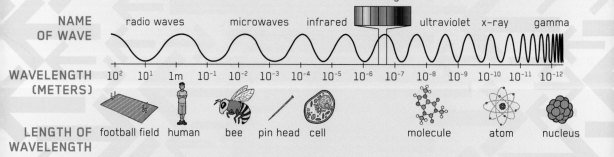

NAME OF WAVE	radio waves		microwaves		infrared			visible light	ultraviolet	x-ray	gamma

| WAVELENGTH (METERS) | 10^2 | 10^1 | 1m | 10^{-1} | 10^{-2} | 10^{-3} | 10^{-4} | 10^{-5} | 10^{-6} | 10^{-7} | 10^{-8} | 10^{-9} | 10^{-10} | 10^{-11} | 10^{-12} |

| LENGTH OF WAVELENGTH | football field | human | | bee | pin head | cell | | | | molecule | | atom | | nucleus |

Albert Einstein
(1879-1955)

What do *you* do with your spare time? In 1905, 26-year-old Albert Einstein patiently read through piles of patent applications at work. In the evenings, he figured out that light acts like tiny particles and won a Nobel Prize. He explained how the drunken, "random-walk" patterns made by pollen particles in water could prove, at least mathematically, that atoms existed. He also devised his special theory of relativity, which says that everybody sees light moving at the same speed and uses the same laws of physics whether they're moving steadily or standing still. This leads to strange but true observations such as clocks ticking more slowly and flattening from front to back on speeding jet planes. And don't forget his $E = mc^2$: this brief equation tells you how much energy any mass is packing.

Later, Einstein's general theory of relativity observed that gravity pulling one way is equivalent to acceleration in the other direction—and since motion warps measurements, so must gravity. This got him seeing space-time as dented by objects in the universe, with gravity's pull being the bending in between. Throughout his years both in Europe and the United States, he studied quantum physics, predicted a new state of matter, and searched for a unified theory of the universe. He didn't find it, but nobody else has, either.

A look around the room showed me framed cartoon cels of old Disney characters, posters and storyboards from my favorite comics, and drawings from manga books and graphic novels. "Look, no art!" I flicked off the light switch, making them all disappear. Everyone laughed. Except Liam.

I turned it back on when I heard the guard's heavy steps heading our way. "Very funny," said Liam. "Don't get us thrown out. I've got a big story waiting next door."

are we on the same wavelength here?

A light wave is a transverse wave, which means it moves like ripples across the sea: it jiggles in a repeating pattern at right angles while it travels forward. Imagine a duck bobbing up and down in the waves near a shore. The distance between the pattern repeats is the wavelength. Frequency is how many waves pass by each second. Amplitude? It tells you how strong the wave is.

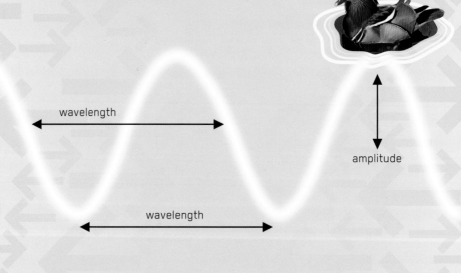

wavelength

wavelength

amplitude

First wave, now particle? A particle of light is called a photon. With no mass and no volume, a photon's kind of freaky. And light's identity crisis is worse than you think. It stays mixed up until you look at it—and then, whether it becomes a wave or a particle depends on how you measure it. Audrey says even Nobel Prize winners don't really get it. That's just the way things work in the quantum world, where things get really, really small and truly bizarre.

"Actually, Jeremy's got a point," said Audrey. Liam turned to frown at me but hey, I didn't do it on purpose.

"You're cracked," Oscar argued. "The art is there, whether it's dark or not."

"Really?" Audrey threw back. "How do you know it's art, if you can't see it?"

Oscar gave an exaggerated sigh. "Fine. Enlighten us," he said sarcastically.

"What's to discuss? Light is light, pure and simple," stated Liam firmly. "It's like air— just there."

"It's not as simple as you think," said Audrey. "Physicists couldn't make up their minds for the longest time whether light is a wave or a particle. Now they know it's both. You can think of light as either energy particles or energy waves."

"That doesn't make sense," I said. "How can light be both?"

"Light acts like both a wave and a particle," replied Audrey. "It moves in a straight line and bounces off shiny barriers, like a ball banked off the side of a pool table."

"That's the particle part?" asked Oscar.

"Yes," answered Audrey. "But light also spreads out, like waves rippling from a rock dropped in a pond. And you can fully blend two different beams of light, something you can't do with particles."

Oscar was impatient. "So go on, what's the deal with light and art?"

"The deal is, you can't see art or anything else without the physics of light," said Audrey. "It starts when light waves from an object hit your eye."

"In case you haven't noticed, none of this stuff is glowing," Oscar pointed out.

"Let me back up," said Audrey. "Some of the light from the sun or a lamp reflects off things around it—art, trees, people, planets, whatever. From there, waves from the visible slice of the spectrum enter your eye and refract, or bend, going through the cornea and lens. That's how we see." Audrey rummaged in her bag for a pen and scrap of paper to show us. "These parts of the eye focus the waves, which I'm drawing as rays, so that they form an image on the screen made by the retina at the back of your eye."

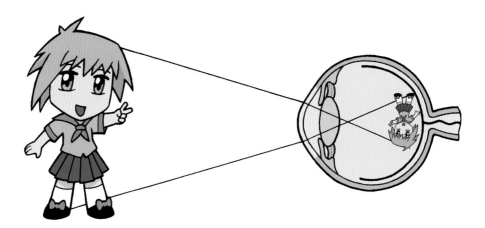

reflection, just light bouncing off stuff. Then there's refraction, which is more like bend- ing. Light travels at different speeds in different materials. In a vacuum, light clocks in at over 1 billion kilometers (almost 0.7 billion miles) an hour: that's 8 minutes for the 150-million-kilometer (93-million-mile) run from Earth to the sun! It's slightly slower in air, and slower still in water. So light crossing from air into water, or anything else, is forced to slow down. If it slants in, you get refraction: one part of the light wave slows down before the rest, and steers the whole light wave off course. How much slowing and bending is set by the material's refractive index, a number comparing the speed of light in a vacuum and the speed of light in the material; the higher the refractive index, the slower light goes and the more it bends.

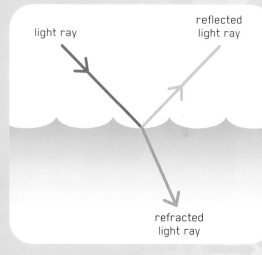

light ray

reflected light ray

refracted light ray

Liam smirked, tilting his head at the inverted chibi in Audrey's sketch. She wasn't bad at drawing those funny manga mini-characters. "Last time I checked," Liam said, "the world was right-side up."

"I'm not saying it isn't," replied Audrey. "Your brain flips it automatically."

Liam opened and closed his mouth, like he wanted to disagree but didn't know how.

Oscar still had a problem. "If everything we see is just reflected light," he argued, pointing to a poster showing the Incredible Hulk, "then explain how plain white light ends up colored green on *him*."

"First, white light isn't white," said Audrey.

"You're telling us white isn't white." Oscar crossed his arms and waited.

"Second," she said, "the Incredible Hulk's skin is every color except green."

Silence.

"You know how electromagnetic radiation comes in different wavelengths? Well, the wavelengths in the visible part of the spectrum show up as bands of color, from violet to red," began Audrey. "White light is really a mix of all the colors—you can see it when sunlight is split through raindrops into a rainbow."

"All right, I'll give you that point," said Oscar. "What about the Hulk—the one that's *not* green?"

"Well, the ink used on the Hulk part of the poster absorbs almost all the visible wavelengths except the greenish ones, so those are what reflect to your eyes," said Audrey. "Your retinas have rod cells to sense light and three kinds of cone cells that are tuned to wavelengths in the blue, green, or red bands. So when photons of green light reflect off the picture, green-sensing cones absorb them and signal 'green' to the brain."

"News flash for you," said Liam. "This is a multicolor universe, as in more than red, blue, and green."

"Well, of course," responded Audrey. "But we can't have

presenting

before your very eyes (or not), the world's first invisibility cloak! In 2007, researchers used something called plasmon technology to create a cloaking device that steers visible light waves past and back around an object, just like the Fantastic Four's Invisible Woman bends light with her mind. Your eyes think the light is traveling straight, so you're tricked into believing nothing's there. Don't get too excited, though. Nobody's fitting under this cloak: it's smaller than a grain of sand and made of stiff plastic and gold film arranged in tiny rings. And even if you could fit, it wouldn't hide more than two of your three dimensions.

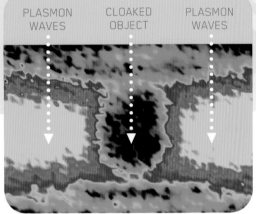

PLASMON WAVES · CLOAKED OBJECT · PLASMON WAVES

different cones for each of the 10 million or so shades of color we see. Each shade is a different mix of wavelengths that are sensed by different cones in combination."

She looked at Oscar, who was quiet. "I think he's 'absorbing' the information," I joked. "Or just 'reflecting' on it?"

Liam didn't seem to appreciate my joke. "Let's go—they must be done by now." He jerked his head back the way we came.

Through the doorway, I could see the room had emptied, except for two men, still standing in front of the suspect painting. Now I could see it clearly: a canvas splattered all over with drips of color. "It looks like someone threw paint at it."

"Yes, but with such *control*," said Oscar, with an important nod. "For those who understand abstract art, Jackson Pollock's work is amazing. Really valuable, too, if it's not fake. But it's almost impossible to forge a Pollock."

"Are you kidding?" I said. "Anyone can dribble paint from a can." Not that I really meant it—I just wanted a reaction from Oscar.

I didn't get it though, because Liam shushed us as we walked into the room. The men were still talking in worried tones. "What now, Mr. Sanger?" asked one man. "The owner needs a decision."

"I know," the curator responded in a despairing voice. "But the art scholar and art historian we brought in both seemed certain that this is a Pollock creation. An equally renowned historian and a highly respected dealer don't agree. It was picked up originally at a yard sale, so nobody knows where it came from. The board has been quite clear, though: they will not risk the gallery's reputation." Mr. Sanger paced in front of the painting. "If the best Pollock experts in the world can't agree, how can we be sure it's not fake?"

Audrey interrupted. "Physics can help you."

Liam stepped quickly in front of her and said, "Pay no attention. Small children...always talking nonsense, you know. I'm from *The Daily Citizen*. If I can have a few minutes of your time—"

But both men were intrigued. "I'll be holding a press conference shortly," said Mr. Sanger to Liam, "but if this young lady can help me, you can have an exclusive on the result." He paused. "She *is* with you, isn't she?"

Liam was quick to confirm. I smothered a laugh.

"Talk to some of the physicists in town for the conference," suggested Audrey. "An expert in spectroscopy can run some tests."

Seeing puzzled looks, she added, "Spectroscopy looks at how a sample absorbs or sends back different kinds of light, and uses the information to figure out what the sample might be made of. It could tell you if this painting's too new to be old—like, if the artist died a long time ago, he couldn't have used paints invented in the last 20 years."

"I remember reading about this!" said Mr. Sanger, snapping his finger. "It's like fingerprinting. We send paint samples out to a lab, get the patterns back, and have experts match them up with pigment patterns on file at one of the national art centers."

Oscar was horrified. "You'd scrape paint off a potential masterpiece?"

"Well, most methods require very small samples, and I believe...," Mr. Sanger frowned, trying to remember, "some instruments use portable scanners. I'll contact the scientists right away." Mr. Sanger beamed, then turned to Liam. "Once the results are in and we make a decision, we'll let you know first—but you make sure this young lady gets the credit she deserves."

Liam nodded, but looked slightly sick. Oscar, on the other hand, seemed pretty impressed. "Fingerprinting, forgery...this is straight out of *CSI*! Maybe there *is* a place for physics in art."

"Oh, give me a break," Liam grumbled as we left the room. Audrey's smile was triumphant, but all she did was tell Oscar he should come to the public meeting later. As for me, I normally loved spy stuff, but not right then. Our mission was in serious jeopardy, now that Oscar *and* the baseball team had bailed.

I glanced at Liam. "Great. Oscar's no good to us now. But at least he's just one person."

I spoke too soon, though. Oscar left us to meet his buddies on the gallery steps. As we walked away, I heard him say, "You should have been there—we're investigating this huge forgery ring and calling in forensic physicists to examine the evidence! Wouldn't it be cool if they put a spectroscopy lab in the new physics building?"

"That boy's been corrupted." Liam's voice was grim. "Come on. We're heading to the park. It's almost time for my next interview." He glanced at Audrey, and dropped his voice before telling me, "You can work on some new recruits."

At the same time, Audrey said in my other ear, "Who's he hoping to brainwash there?"

I shrugged, not looking at her. How do double agents get past the guilt? "You've heard of Valerie Ryan, haven't you?"

"The singer?" Audrey squealed, and for a minute I could believe she was normal.

"Yeah, well, she grew up here...and is back visiting. She had this idea to get some kids playing on her next CD," I said. We could see a bunch of kids with instruments and music stands in one corner of the park. "So all those guys are auditioning. And the rest are fans, I guess."

"Finally, real artists," announced Liam with satisfaction, "or at least, artists in training. Those art gallery fellows, they don't know the difference between science and art. But listen to that— pure, youthful artistry, untainted by physics!"

Liam's mood had changed during the walk. He was sure of himself again. Not me. Audrey's success so far was making me nervous. And I remembered last fall, how Sam had shown us all that math in music. But that was a whole other debate, wasn't it? Snap out of it, I told myself. Focus. If you want that summer fair, then get back to the mission at hand!

"There she is...Valerie Ryan," said Liam. "Left town years ago," he continued, gazing at the small, dark-haired woman. "Poor girl... she was devastated when I ended our relationship. But obviously the suffering brought her music to a new level. She's an international star now."

The last notes of the theme from *The Simpsons* faded away. "Valerie!" Liam called eagerly.

The woman looked up. "Oh, hello. You must be the reporter the newspaper sent..."

"Valerie, it's good to see you! It's me…Liam? From college?" He let his voice trail off, embarrassed.

"Oh, of course," she said blankly. All the kids turned to listen.

"Well, um, if this is a good time, why don't we get started," said Liam, pretending not to hear the snickers. "People say you have a magic touch, whether you pick up the microphone or one of the many instruments you've mastered. How do you make such beautiful music—or is that a fair question? Music is a gift that transcends explanation." He gave Audrey a lofty, but loaded, smile.

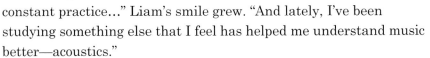

"I'm grateful for my gift, but can't take full credit," responded Valerie. "Much of it I owe to great teachers and constant practice…" Liam's smile grew. "And lately, I've been studying something else that I feel has helped me understand music better—acoustics."

Liam looked bewildered, but Audrey wore a look of glee. Why, I found out as Valerie went on. "Acoustics is the study of sound, and the only difference between noise and music, after all, is just the right mix of sound waves."

"Waves? As in the *physics* kind?" I asked. In spite of my own panic, I had to admit that the look on Liam's face was worth a day in physics class—just one, though.

Audrey jumped in, saying, "That's right. Almost like light waves, but not quite. Sound waves are longitudinal waves." Maybe the confused faces around her were a hint. "When a wave, any wave, ripples, the energy it carries temporarily upsets the stuff it goes through, right?"

Not waiting for an answer, she quickly borrowed a Slinky from a little girl she had spotted nearby and shoved one end at me. I took it, not really knowing what else to do, as she walked away with the other end, saying, "Well, light is a transverse wave, so it disturbs whatever it's traveling through at right angles to the way the wave itself heads. It's like this—watch." She gave the toy a series of sideways jerks.

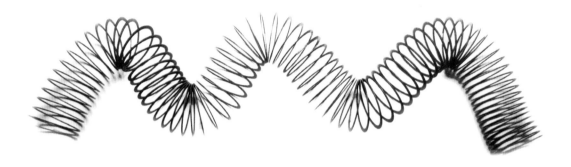

"But sound is a longitudinal wave, and here's the difference: both the disturbance and the wave go in the same direction." Audrey stopped wiggling the Slinky. Instead, she gathered the first few coils, then pulled back and released them, in a move that reminded me of pinball. The coils bunched and spread out along the length of the toy.

"I don't hear a thing." Liam stood with his arms crossed.

those speed traps! Sound's no slacker, except in the vacuum of space, where the absence of vibration-carrying particles pretty much stops it cold. On Earth, in air at regular temperature and pressure, sound goes 343 meters per second (1,125 feet per second). Gearing up, it roars up to about 1,500 m/s (4,900 ft/s) in water and to about 5,200 m/s (17,000 ft/s) in steel. But that's a cakewalk compared to this: the element beryllium (an expensive material with aerospace and military uses) transmits sound waves at a blistering 12,900 m/s (42,300 ft/s). That's really putting pedal to the metal.

"The Slinky's just a model to show how sound waves move," said Valerie, turning to the cello next to her. "Watch and listen. When I pluck this string, it vibrates—it crams the nearest air molecules forward, then pulls them back. Every jammed region of air does the same thing to its neighbors. You can't see it, but a pattern ripples away, made of squashed zones, called compressions, next to empty zones, called rarefactions—just like coils down a Slinky."

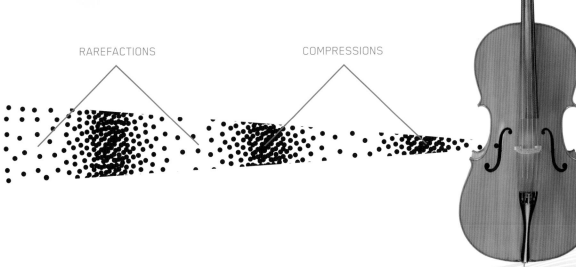

RAREFACTIONS   COMPRESSIONS

"But that sounds like none of the air molecules go anywhere—they just spring back," I argued. "So what's getting to your ear?"

"Energy," answered Audrey. "When that pattern of energy vibrates your ear drum, it sets the tiny bones in your ear moving, which transfers the vibration to a fluid. Tiny hairs touching the fluid pick up the motion and send messages describing the sound to your brain."

JEREMY WRESTLES WITH THE WEIRD STUFF...

Spy kids unite! Cell phones featuring the Mosquitotone offer parent- and teacher-proof communication. The annoying cell-phone ring whines at 14,400 hertz, too high for aging ears to hear, but well within kid range. Sound frequency is measured in hertz, with 1 hertz (Hz) equaling one compression (or rarefaction) pounding your ear each second. Normal humans (including parents) hear in the 20- to 20,000-hertz range. Above that, sound goes ultrasonic—we can't stand it, but bats and dolphins are good to 200,000 hertz. Subnormal sounds are infrasonic, best left to pigeons, who like it low, down to 0.1 hertz. Talk about technology turning against you, though. Some shopkeepers blast the Mosquitotone nonstop outside their shops to send delinquents a message: buzz off!

"So vibrations make noise," snapped Liam. "Are you telling me these 'wavy vibrations,'" he challenged, wriggling his fingers in the air, "make actual music?"

"It's like Valerie said earlier," Audrey replied. "Music comes from the right combination of waves. Each musical note is a wave with its own frequency. For example, the A above middle C is 440 hertz.

Our brains match high frequencies to high-pitched sounds and low frequencies to low pitches. Stringing different frequencies together gets you a nice melody."

A tune floated out from behind us, the theme from the movie *Star Wars*—only not quite. Jen was picking it out with one hand on the piano. "There you go, a melody," she said. Of course she'd be here. Jen's crazy about music—plays a bunch of instruments and sings, too.

"Sorry, not impressed." Liam sneered at Jen before turning to Valerie. "If that's physics in action, you can't tell me it's the secret of your success."

"That's just the beginning," she replied. "Physics lets us mix sound waves in interesting ways to get music. It's deliberate interference."

Huh? "Who wants to listen to interference?" I said.

"When sound waves from separate instruments run into each other and merge into a new pattern of loud and quiet spots, it's called interfer- ence," Valerie continued. "Also, the different frequencies overlap. If the new, combined wave vibrates in a regular, repeating pattern, it'll sound good. If it's a jumbled mess, you get noise."

"Like this?" said Jen, knocking over the music stand beside her.

"Exactly," said Valerie. "Doesn't it sound awful? It's sending out a hit-and-miss mix of sound waves."

"So notes that sound especially nice together create good vibration patterns?" asked Jen.

Valerie nodded. Leaning over Jen at her piano, she ran her finger across the sheet music. "Composers know this. They choose good combinations, like this first bit where you play C and G together a lot." Jen played through the piece with both hands. Now that sounded like the *Star Wars* theme I remembered! Someone's cello and a flute joined in.

I couldn't help applauding when they finished, but at an elbow from Liam, I stopped. "Well, you've got to admit—interference never sounded so good."

"Hey," growled Liam. "Are you working with me, or against me?"

"Keep it down," I hissed. "Undercover, remember?" Rats. Audrey was looking my way.

She turned quickly back to Valerie and the kids. "You guys sounded great," she said, smiling. "But your instruments get some credit, too."

"About time we changed the subject," muttered Liam.

"Not exactly," said Audrey. "Musical instruments are designed for interference. When you blow into a flute or pluck a guitar string, you start a sound wave. The instrument bounces the wave back on itself, like a mirror, so it interferes with itself."

"The resulting pattern looks like it's standing still, so we call it a standing wave pattern," said Valerie. She turned some sheet music over and made a quick sketch.

STANDING WAVE PATTERN

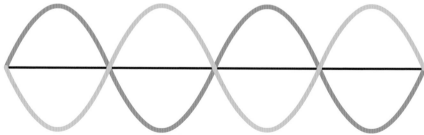

"Every instrument creates these standing waves, and usually a whole bunch at the same time," said Audrey, adding to Valerie's sketch. "They're called harmonics."

1ST HARMONIC   2ND HARMONIC   3RD HARMONIC

"Within any set of harmonics produced, you hear some more than others, depending on the size, shape, and material of the instrument body. The blend helps give instruments what musicians call their timbre. For a flute, you hear only one harmonic," said Valerie, blowing a long, clear note. "That's why it sounds so pure." She pointed at Jen, who promptly picked up a tuba and blew a drawn-out blast. "But the tuba has a mix of harmonics for a nice, rich tone."

"And this happens for each note?" asked Jen.

"Yes," replied Audrey. "When you change notes, you're changing the frequencies of the whole harmonic set."

pump up the volume, and you up the intensity. Measured in decibels, loudness describes intensity—how powerfully sound energy pounds your eardrum. When two almost identical waves travel the same space and interfere, the combined intensity gets a good beat going. And speaking of beats, are catchy tunes contagious? A vibrating guitar string gets its sound box shaking and the air molecules inside it moshing the same way, for louder sound. When the vibe from one object matches the natural frequency of another, resonance sets the second thing shaking.

"Changing frequencies doesn't sound like something you can do with just your fingers," commented Jen, looking down at hers.

"You can," said Valerie, picking up a guitar, "and quite easily." She plucked a string, then pressed down on a fret and plucked it again.

"A short vibrating string gives a higher pitch than a long one!" said Jen. "I knew that, but not why. So the short string vibrates at a higher frequency? What about instruments without strings?"

"In instruments like flutes, air vibrates inside the long column made by the instrument's body," said Valerie. "By opening up holes, you shorten the length that's available and you force a higher frequency."

"Let's get back to the interview, shall we?" Liam rushed to say. "There's only one question on everybody's mind, I'm sure: what brings an international star like you back home?"

Valerie smiled. "I love it here, of course. And I'm looking for young talent to feature on my next CD…"

"You're looking for dedicated, focused kids, then," interrupted Liam.

"Like me!" said Jen. "I practice at least an hour every day, even during the summer."

"Then there's no way you have time for those physics camps," I said.

JEREMY WRESTLES WITH THE WEIRD STUFF…

Wait a minute. I thought deep space was silent. But Audrey's been going on about a singing black hole. In 2003, NASA's Chandra X-Ray Observatory detected a deep-bass broadcast from a super-massive black hole in the group of galaxies called the Perseus Cluster, 25 million light-years away. Actually, it's no song—the black hole belts out just one note: a B-flat, 57 octaves below middle C and a million billion times lower than anything we'll ever hear. So how did those space scientists hear it? They didn't. They *saw* it, in the form of x-rays picked up by the observatory's detectors. I knew black holes were great at sucking things in. What I didn't know was that they also spin stuff around, heat it up, and spit it out—spewing loads of energy in the form of x-rays and setting up giant ripples of sound in the process.

Valerie gave Liam and me a cold look. "I didn't finish telling you why I came home," she said. "I'm also one of the speakers at the physics symposium, and I'm teaching some of their kids' classes." She smiled at Audrey and the others. "They're going to be fun, so do come. And I hope you'll support the new physics building at the public meeting tonight, too."

Liam ground his teeth and snapped the pencil he held in frustration. I was beginning to panic. We were really sunk now. Those kids all loved Valerie Ryan and her singing. They'd do anything for her, and we all knew it.

SNAP!

hey, chill.

Yes, you, the ice cream. Acoustics researchers Steven Garrett and Matthew Poese invented an environmentally friendly way to freeze ice-cream maker Ben & Jerry's frozen treats. The fire hydrant-sized, thermoacoustic freezer runs on less power than regular freezers and uses only sound waves and harmless gases. Inside a shell of steel, a souped-up loudspeaker attached to an ice-cream cabinet screams for ice cream—at 195 decibels! Outside, not a peep. The vibration from the sound waves switches between squeezing the gas to heat it and expanding the gas to cool it. A steel screen removes the heat produced by squeezing, while the cold gas from expansion is used to cool the freezer.

Marie Curie
(1867-1934)

Marie Curie's love of physics brought her romance, fame, two Nobel prizes—and tragedy. Born Maria Skłodowska, Marie's early university years were difficult, with studies snatched secretly in defiance of Polish laws against education for women. Later, she had little money to live on while studying at the famous Sorbonne in Paris, France, where she met her husband, physicist Pierre Curie. Despite the hardship, she emerged with degrees in physics and mathematics. Together, the Curies spent years studying radioactivity (discovered by Henri Becquerel) in a cold, leaky shed. The outcome: two new radioactive elements, which they named polonium and radium. Marie Curie became the first European woman to earn a doctorate, Pierre was made professor at the Sorbonne, and both shared a Nobel Prize with Becquerel.

Then, tragedy struck. Pierre was killed by a horse-drawn wagon, leaving Marie Curie to receive new, bittersweet honors alone: a laboratory and a new unit for radiation level, both named "curie," and a second Nobel Prize. During World War I, Marie supplied and operated mobile x-ray units on French battlefields and donated radon (radioactive gas) to destroy diseased tissue. Yet as radiation became crucial to medicine and other fields, over-exposure was discovered to be deadly. Too late: Marie Curie died from aplastic anemia, caused by a lifetime of exposure to radiation.

Liam stomped to the far side of the park, where he flung himself under a tree and dared the squirrels to bother him. I followed. No telling what he'd do to the animals.

I was feeling a little bummed myself. Our anti-physics campaign was fizzling big-time. I snuck a glance at Liam, who seemed suddenly cheerful. "Uh, Liam? What's up? What's the plan now? You've got to admit the gallery thing was impressive, the team thinks physics is their ace-in-the-hole, and with Valerie and all those star-struck kids…if they all come to the meeting—"

"Let them come. Phase II of the plan kicks in an hour before the meeting," said Liam. "And this corner of the park is the perfect place for me to concentrate on fine-tuning it. I don't see anything you could call physics here."

By this time, Audrey had wandered over, too. "Feeling better?" she asked.

"I'm just fine, no thanks to you," said Liam. "A little relaxation in the park works wonders. Nothing but sun and stillness, some bird song, a pond…"

"You can't separate physics from nature," said Audrey, hiding a smile. "That bird song is an army of air particles dive-bombing your eardrums at the speed of sound. The sunlight? Energy-charged photons, fallout from the sun's nuclear-fusion oven. And the waves in that pond…"

"Now you stop that!" A vein started throbbing in Liam's temple and he clambered to his feet. "Nature...is...natural. Nothing's predictable, and there are no rules!"

"Hate to tell you this," Audrey said, "but nature follows rules, too, especially where energy's involved."

Rules? It just gets better and better, I thought.

"There's one rule you've got to remember: you can't make energy, and you can't destroy it," said Audrey. "That's the law of conservation of energy."

what's energy?

Energy is what makes things happen. And work and heat are ways of making them happen—they're processes for transferring energy. Work is done only when you move something over a distance. So pressing a single piano key is work, but failing miserably to budge a 250-kilogram (550-pound) piano isn't. Heat is energy flow driven by differences in temperature: that's energy leaving your hot and sweaty self for the cold pool water you dive into, to cool off after your failed piano-pushing attempt. Put another way, heat is action shifting from high energy to low—in hot objects, atoms are bustling; in cold ones, they're in slo-mo.

"But that's bogus. We eat up loads of energy every day," I argued. "I can't even ask for a ride somewhere without my dad telling me the world's going to run out of gas."

"You're talking about energy sources," said Audrey. "Sources might get used up, but the energy in them lives on."

"Okay, but then where does the energy go?" I asked. "And if you can't create it, where does it come from?"

"It's like recycling. The total amount of energy in the universe never changes, but it gets shifted through different forms," said Audrey. "See that skateboarder? At the top of the half-pipe, all his energy is potential—it's stored and ready to roll. The second he moves, his potential energy starts turning into kinetic energy. That's energy in action, and it carries him up the other side to become potential again. He's transforming energy nonstop the whole time he's in the half-pipe."

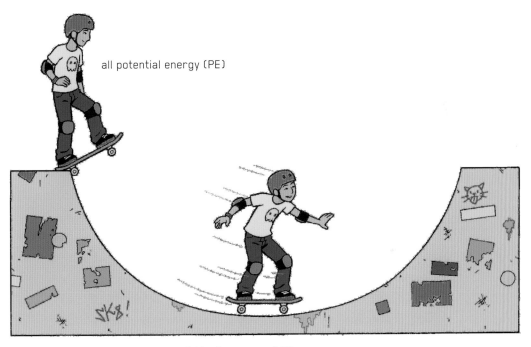

all potential energy (PE)

all kinetic energy (KE)

She was pointing at Nick. You never see him without his skateboard, except maybe in class, because the teachers take it from him. "But look at how he has to pump," I said. "If the energy just keeps transforming back and forth, shouldn't he go forever *without* pumping?"

the laws

of thermodynamics (the science that studies how energy moves, through work and heat) are the ultimate guide to what's hot, what's not. The first law reminds us that the total energy in the universe is conserved, and says that the only way any stationary object in the universe can change its own energy is by doing work or transferring heat. The second law says that energy has this way of spreading only from high energy to low, until it's the same all around. So ice cream never unmelts because it takes more energy to hold it frozen than leave it liquid. The third law says that at absolute zero (-273°C/ -460°F), there's nothing: no heat, no molecules moving. There's also no chance of ever getting that chilly, though scientists have come close. The zeroth law—discovered last, but

so basic it should come first—says if two things are each at the same temperature as a third, then the two must also be at the same temperature.

"Not in real life. The friction between the wheels of his skateboard and the concrete turns some of the kinetic energy into heat," said Audrey. "But energy's still conserved: heat counts in the total, too."

Before Audrey could say more, it started raining. "What a shame, rain," sang out Liam. "Lecture's over—run for cover!"

We ran to the closest tree and stood under it. But nothing could douse Audrey's enthusiasm. "We were talking about heat," she said, rain dripping down her nose. "Well, heat flow's responsible for a lot of weather."

Liam started laughing. "Now you're going too far...heat causing this cold, miserable storm?"

"Miserable is right," said Nick, ducking under the branches with his skateboard.

"According to her," said Liam, jerking his head in Audrey's direction, "it's the fault of physics, heat physics or some other silly thing we'd be better off without."

"It's called atmospheric thermodynamics," said Audrey. "Weather is just fallout from heat on the move. It all starts at the sun: everyday, its energy breaks through the upper atmosphere and the cloud cover to warm up the earth's surface. But the heating's uneven. Land heats up faster than water; dark areas warm better than light ones…"

"Everyone knows that. That's why we all head to the beach on hot days, to bake on the sand and cool off in the water," said Nick. "Except me, of course. It's kind of hard to skateboard on sand."

if you can't take the heat, get out…

Heat has three ways of transporting energy: radiation, conduction, and convection. In radiation, it sails directly across space as electromagnetic waves emitted by hot, jittery particles. Then there's conduction, where thermal energy passes hand to hand—uh, make that molecule to molecule—by direct contact at close range. Metallic solids conduct heat best, which is why we often use copper pots for cooking.

When heat moves with a fluid (liquid or gas), you've got convection. A warm fluid becomes less dense than its surroundings and rises, like steam from a cup of cocoa or blobs in a lava lamp.

Audrey doesn't know Nick like I do—to him, everything's about skateboarding. She paused but went on, "So all over the earth, these warm areas are heating up the air directly overhead. The added energy spreads the colliding air molecules out. Because the air becomes less dense, it floats up and leaves a gap that cool air sweeps in to fill."

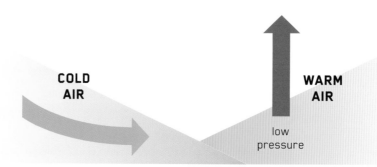

COLD
AIR

WARM
AIR

low
pressure

"Air's pretty pushy, butting in wherever there's space," I commented. "Like with the baseball."

Audrey nodded. "Air is always moving to balance out pressures. Wind comes from air shifting from high- to low-pressure areas; the bigger the pressure difference, the stronger the wind. There's more to it, though: wind is slowed down by the friction of air scrubbing everything on the ground, and it's forced to turn around hills and forests."

"Just like me," said Nick. "Can't skate fast over gravel, and there's always stuff to swerve around on the ground."

"And then," said Audrey, "there's the Coriolis effect: the earth spins fastest at the equator and slowest near the poles, but the wind doesn't change speed to match. So it ends up swerving— to the right in the northern hemisphere, to the left in the southern half."

Audrey gouged a rough picture in the mud with a stick. "Put it all together, and you end up with this."

The rain filled and threatened to erase Audrey's muddy grooves. My shoes were soaking it all in, too. "It's not staying dry under here. Where's it all coming from?"

"The clouds, obviously," said Liam. "It's not rocket science."

"Just atmospheric science," Audrey reminded him. "Rain falls when enough cloud droplets—a lot, like a million or so—stick together to make a raindrop that's heavy enough to fall."

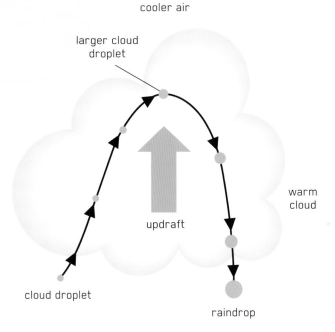

cooler air

larger cloud droplet

warm cloud

updraft

cloud droplet

raindrop

"What do you mean, cloud droplets?" Nick asked.

"Clouds are a collection of tiny water drops. The water in warm air exists as a gas, or water vapor. But as warm air rises, it spreads out and becomes cooler," explained Audrey. "Cold air can't hold as much water vapor, so the extra vapor condenses, changing from gas into water, and forms droplets around tiny floating particles like clay or salt."

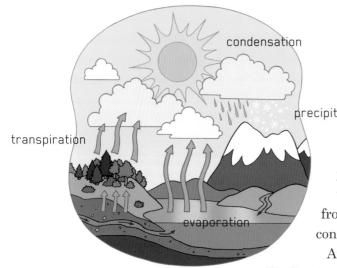

condensation

precipitation

transpiration

evaporation

"I don't see where the water comes from in the first place, before it gets in the air," I said.

"Pretty much everywhere: oceans, lakes, rivers, other water bodies…plants, animals, you…," listed Audrey. "All that water evaporates—or transpires, from plants—into the atmosphere and condenses back down again."

At last! The rain was stopping.

"Well, wherever it came from today, it's finally gone," I said, spraying water off my head like a dog. We emerged from beneath the branches.

JEREMY WRESTLES WITH THE WEIRD STUFF…

Every so often, a snow day does come in handy, like when I haven't done my homework. What I'd give for power over the weather! But even I couldn't come up with the bizarre stuff real physicists have dreamed up to fight global warming. How about giant eggbeaters frothing seawater into salt-water droplets, so clouds can form to reflect the sun's rays back into space? A bazillion tiny aluminum balloons shot into the atmosphere would do the job nicely, too, or adjustable mirrors that are 2,000 kilometers (1,240 miles) wide, up among the stars. Those are real suggestions by serious scientists, I swear. If you don't believe me, check with the National Center for Atmospheric Research—research groups like this one make it their mission to sort out what works from what doesn't.

"Yes, finally," said Audrey, with a glance at the sky. "At some point, cold clouds sink and drop, where they get squeezed by the higher-pressure surroundings and warm up. Then the whole cloud of droplets evaporates away, or changes into gas. If it clears up, we'll see stars tonight."

"Stargazing would suit me just fine," said Liam. "Anything to get away from your insistence that we can't escape physics."

"Yeah, stars have nothing to do with physics or us," I agreed.

"Stars have everything to do with both," said Audrey. "For starters, we're both made of the same thing: atoms."

"Everyone knows that atoms are the building blocks of the universe," said Liam. "More knowledgeable folks, like me, also know that an atom is made of electrons circling a nucleus made of protons and neutrons."

"And he *failed* physics," I offered.

"Your information's a little out of date," said Audrey. "Physicists learned long ago that electrons don't simply circle the nucleus— they can be anywhere in the surrounding territory. And particles 100,000 times smaller than the atom exist: for example, electrons are just one type of particle called leptons, and protons and neutrons are made up of other particles called quarks."

"Assembly not required, right?" I joked.

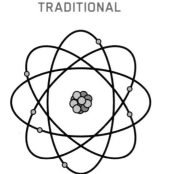

TRADITIONAL

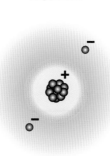

MODERN

"Luckily," said Audrey, "most atoms don't just fall apart. They're held together by strong, weak, and electromagnetic forces."

"Okay," said Nick. "So deep down, we're all the same, whether we're stars or people. But what else do stars have to do with anything?"

"Lots," said Audrey, "including how our world began—and how it might end."

"Those are pretty big questions," said Liam. "You're sadly mistaken if you think physics has all the answers!"

"Most astrophysicists believe the universe was created in the Big Bang—an ultra-hot expansion about 14 billion years ago," said Audrey. "The whole universe blasted outward from a super-dense clump of energy billions and billions of times smaller than a proton."

the standard model of the atom:

The Universe in Three Easy Steps. As a manual for building just about everything, the Standard Model works pretty well. The parts list is short: six kinds of quarks (up, down, charm, strange, top, and bottom), six types of leptons (electron, electron neutrino, muon, muon neutrino, tau, and tau neutrino), and four kinds of force-carrying particles (gluons, photons, and W and Z bosons). The steps are simple, too. Make protons and neutrons by gluing quarks into groups with strong force. Build the nucleus, binding protons and neutrons with more strong force. Finally, add electrons, using electromagnetic force. *Voila*: an atom. Not bad for a beginner. Of course, things do break. Take radioactive atoms, whose construction is based on weak forces: their nuclei fall apart constantly, ejecting particles and energy through a very slow, really random process called tunneling.

Erwin Schrödinger (1887–1961)
Werner Karl Heisenberg (1901–1976)
Paul Adrien Maurice Dirac (1902–1984)

The battle was on: Whose theory of quantum mechanics would reign supreme? Who would solve the problems left by an incomplete model of the atom? The time: the mid-1920s; the place: Europe; the opponents: Heisenberg and Schrödinger.

Werner Heisenberg had youth on his side, and his theoretical skills were honed to perfection. His weapon of choice: matrix mechanics, a theory used to calculate a particle's motion based on light emitted and absorbed by atoms. Later, he came up with his uncertainty principle, about the impossibility of accurate quantum measurements.

Erwin Schrödinger's advantage was experience. Born in Vienna, Austria, Schrödinger was almost 40 when he thought of explaining electron movement with a wave equation. He also dreamed up the famous Schrödinger's cat paradox, an imaginary experiment involving radioactive atoms and a cat that's alive and dead at the same time.

Into the fray stepped Paul Dirac, a quiet, brilliant Englishman about Heisenberg's age. Dirac defused the battle by proving that Schrödinger's and Heisenberg's warring versions said exactly the same thing—just differently. He went on to link quantum mechanics to special relativity, with his famous equation describing particles moving, with spin, at near-light speed.

Did they have anything in common? All three won a Nobel Prize for physics—Dirac and Schrödinger shared one in 1933, while Heisenberg won in 1932—and all three are called the founders of quantum mechanics.

To figure out the gi-normous universe, physicists think puny: they examine subatomic particles and use giant machines, the bigger the better, to do it. Take the Large Hadron Collider (LHC), located in Switzerland. Inside, 9,300 huge electromagnets and a particle accelerator that is 27 kilometers (17 miles) long are designed to send particles hurtling toward each other at near-light speeds. After the atomic demolition derby, particle detectors weighing up to 12,500 tonnes (13,800 tons) will pick up the pieces. Why such violence? To see what falls out: other particles (as if the 200 known ones aren't enough), and even the possibility of time travel—in theory, LHC collisions can rip wormholes in space-time to connect present to past.

"Ready-made, like a pop-up tent with all the accessories?" snorted Liam. "Ridiculous! If that's the best physics can do..."

Audrey sighed. "Not ready-made. It was seriously hot at first, and only a single force existed. But the universe started cooling, and that force split into four."

"That's not much, just energy and forces," I said. "What about planets and stuff?"

"That came a lot later," said Audrey. "The universe was just minutes old when the first bits of matter, and their antimatter partners, formed from the energy."

"Matter and antimatter are real?" Nick asked. "Cool!"

"Yes, they're particles with the same mass but opposite charges," said Audrey. "When they meet, they annihilate each other and all their mass turns into energy."

"But if all matter and antimatter annihilate and disappear…," said Nick.

"Somehow, we ended up with more matter than antimatter," Audrey explained. "They were quarks, which combined into protons and neutrons. When electrons came along, sometime during the next 10,000 years, we got the simplest elements: hydrogen and helium."

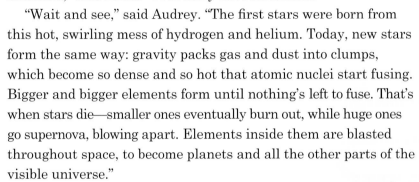

"Aha! You said there were 112 elements," said Liam. "Your story isn't consistent."

"Wait and see," said Audrey. "The first stars were born from this hot, swirling mess of hydrogen and helium. Today, new stars form the same way: gravity packs gas and dust into clumps, which become so dense and so hot that atomic nuclei start fusing. Bigger and bigger elements form until nothing's left to fuse. That's when stars die—smaller ones eventually burn out, while huge ones go supernova, blowing apart. Elements inside them are blasted throughout space, to become planets and all the other parts of the visible universe."

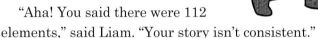

astrophysics,

astronomy, cosmology—what's the difference? Astrophysics is spying and prying into the lives of stars and other celestial stuff to figure out what they're made of and how they work. Cosmology puts them where they belong, in the universe, and looks at how it all came to exist. Put astrophysics and cosmology together, and what do you get? Astronomy.

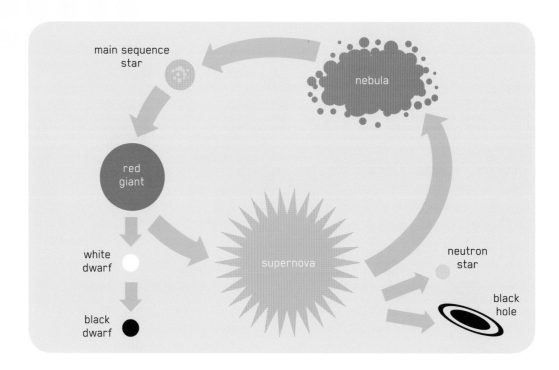

"What do you mean, *visible*?" asked Nick.

"Things we can see, like cars, trees, us, planets—even stars and black holes—are made of atoms and total only about 4 percent of the universe," said Audrey. "Another 23 percent are things we can't see because they don't emit or reflect light. It's like Dust in the book *The Golden Compass*. Physicists know dark matter exists, and they think it might be made of entirely unknown particles."

"That makes only 27 percent," Liam said. "I suppose the rest is *more* stuff nobody's heard of?" His voice was sarcastic.

"Exactly," said Audrey. "The rest is an even bigger mystery called dark energy. In 1998, astronomers noticed that the expansion of the universe was actually speeding up, and dark energy's the reason why."

"Uh...doesn't stretching something really fast rip it?" I said. Not the most comforting thought.

"*You* won't feel a thing," said Audrey. "It'll be 100 billion years before it stretches far enough for all the other galaxies to disappear. Then, the last star will burn out and we'll end up in a black hole."

"That's so cool!" said Nick. "So what's the universe look like right *now*?"

"Nobody knows," said Audrey. "Most physicists agree only that it's flat and it's expanding faster all the time."

Nick wasn't letting her off that easy. "What do they *think*, then?"

"Well, there're lots of theories," she replied. "Einstein's universe was a stretchy rubber sheet, dented by massive objects like the sun. Gravity was the effect felt by other objects traveling the dips and dents between masses. In super-string theory, our universe has six more hidden dimensions, and each particle type is a string or a loop plucked to vibrate in its own special way."

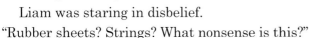

Liam was staring in disbelief. "Rubber sheets? Strings? What nonsense is this?"

Audrey went on without answering him. "In M-theory," she said, "we exist on one 'brane,' which is a separate multidimensional membrane, and share gravity with other branes carrying other universes. My favorite, though, is the many-worlds theory—it's like something out of a comic book. It says that every possible result from every choice exists as a separate universe."

"This physics stuff is better than *Star Trek*," said Nick. I had to admit: this was so weird, it was wild.

" **E** arth to Jeremy." Liam's voice was sarcastic.
"Done? Let's get to the fairgrounds. It's almost time."

Thud. Right. Like Nick, I was caught up in the
weirdness of quarks and cosmology. Unlike Nick, I still had a
mission to complete. As the four of us left the park behind, Liam
was surprisingly upbeat. "I still don't get it," I said in a low
voice. "Audrey's got a lot of kids hooked on this stuff. You're
not worried?"

"No need to be," he replied. "I've got everything under control."

I glanced over my shoulder. Nick had detoured to skate down
some stairs, and Audrey was waiting for him. "Phase II? So tell
me already!" I said.

"Those kids will forget every word she's said when they
remember what they're losing," answered Liam. "What would you
rather do: sweat over thermodynamics or ride the rails on
the roller coaster? Talk about sound waves or scream at the top
of your lungs on a ride? And astronomy? Pretty tame compared
to the fair's fireworks. Think about it."

You know, he was probably right. My heart beat faster at the
sight of my favorite ride, the Devil's Drop of Doom, towering
above everything else…tomorrow, it'd be gone…

All around, kids were arriving, their voices echoing everything
I was thinking.

"Oh man…look at all those crates and tools…," someone said.

"Not the roller coaster...I'll die!" I heard, and "Oh no! The midway's already gone!"

Liam listened with glee. "Showtime," he whispered, putting on a sad face and walking over to the middle of the entry gate. "Children, tomorrow the dismantling of your beloved amusement park begins. I understand your sorrow, even if you don't. What you are losing is no mere summer playground; it's your childhood. This symbol of carefree youth will soon disappear, to be replaced with the serious, adult world of science."

"Don't be ridiculous!" cried Audrey.

Liam gave her a sad smile. "I've arranged for someone to operate the rides one last time, as a farewell tribute, before the public meeting."

What an uncharacteristic stroke of genius—a reminder, just in case anyone had forgotten the thrills.

"So forget physics, let's just have fun!" he shouted. The kids surged through the entrance.

"What do you think is making it fun?" Audrey asked loudly. She watched them go, then followed, looking determined. Liam, Nick, and I trailed behind.

"Bumper cars are great—never mind you guys, *I'll* miss these," said Liam to Angus and Lucas. The whole team was in line for the bumper cars. Jen and Jaime were already climbing into cars.

"Keep watching those bumper cars," said Audrey. "They obey the three laws of motion that Sir Isaac Newton thought up hundreds of years ago. They were major discoveries, and they still describe everything we see moving in the ordinary world."

"Oh-oh. Jen's just stopped in the red car," I said, ignoring the physics lesson. "She's a sitting duck for that blue one." I knew it— the words were barely out when a car sent Jen lurching forward.

"I can use that to show you Newton's first law, about inertia— something anything with mass has," said Audrey. "Inertia causes something that's resting to stay resting until some force gets it going…"

"Like me," I jumped in, "in the morning."

With a roll of her eyes, Audrey continued. "More like how that blue car just jolted Jen. She only lurched, but without friction, the impact would've started her moving. Inertia also keeps something that's already moving going at the same speed and direction until another force changes it. Look, Jen's decided to cruise: she's moving at a steady velocity, meaning she covers the same amount of ground every second in one direction. Nothing changes until—there! Another force just accelerated her right around."

"Accelerated?" I asked. "She didn't speed up, she just spun around."

"Acceleration is any velocity change: speeding up, slowing down, or turning," said Audrey.

"Check out that nut—he's flooring it and going after everybody!" enthused Lucas. "He just got Jaime, and she flew right out of her seat. But that second person he hit, she's just sitting there laughing at him."

Audrey laughed, too. "It's Newton's second law of motion: Force = mass × acceleration. That guy is hitting every car with about the same force, but they accelerate differently because of their different masses. Jaime's small, so she accelerated faster; the bigger girl, just barely."

"And did you see what he did now?" I said. "Rammed into the wall and bounced right off."

"That's Newton's third law of motion: if one thing pushes on another, the second thing pushes back with equal force," said Audrey. "So the wall should return the same force he delivered. Luckily for him, friction and the big bumpers saved him from being hurt."

"Collisions," said Angus. "Aren't they great?"

"Especially for passing along momentum," Audrey added. "Remember the rule about conservation of momentum, from the batting we did?"

I groaned. The team nodded, but Angus asked, "How does it work here?"

"Well, every collision shifts momentum from one car to the other," Audrey continued.

"How much momentum depends on mass and velocity, right?" said Angus. "If we could build up some real speed, we could get some serious crashes going."

Audrey laughed again. "Why do you think bumper cars are built the way they are? The people who make them know their physics. How big a force you feel depends on how fast the momentum is shifted. So they limit the speed on the cars so they can't pack too much momentum in the first place. Then, just in case, the soft bumpers spread the force over a longer time to soften the impact."

"Like the padding in helmets, gloves, and pads," said Angus. "Or airbags in a car."

"Hey, let's get moving," I said. Enough of this momentum business—just like at baseball practice, it didn't take much to con these guys. I didn't need Jen and Jaime, fresh off the bumper cars, joining the discussion either. Besides…so many rides, so little time.

"What's the ride you like so much?" asked Liam. "The Devil's Drop of Doom? I'll give it a go, too." Audrey lifted her eyebrows at this but said nothing. Didn't have to ask me twice. I was there. Liam climbed in beside me, and up the tower we went—probably 13 or 14 stories. "Takes a load off," he said as we reached the top and started the plunge down. "Feels gre—!!"

He didn't look so great when we got off. "I'm fine," he insisted, wobbling a little.

"I get such a rush from this ride," I said. "It's more than just floating…"

"It's like you weigh nothing?" suggested Audrey. "That's exactly what free-fall rides give you—the feeling that you're weightless, even if you're not. Astronauts in orbit feel the same thing."

"I thought astronauts floated because there's no gravity in space," I said.

"Nope. It's because the astronauts and their spacecraft are falling around Earth, just like you were," said Audrey. "Gravity's everywhere. They would weigh nothing only if there was no gravity. So it's really just an apparent weight."

weight

just one minute: better get the difference straight. Remember, mass is the amount of stuff in you. Weight is a force—how strongly gravity pulls you to the center of the earth. Moving to the moon won't change your mass, but it will lessen your weight.

"So when I'm dropping on this ride, my *apparent* weight is zero?" I asked.

"You accelerate down at the same rate gravity pulls," said Audrey. "Your inertia resists this in the opposite direction, and it cancels gravity exactly."

I wasn't getting this, and it must have showed. "Imagine standing on a scale in an elevator," said Audrey. "If you're stopped, the scale shows your normal weight. When the elevator accelerates up, you push down harder on the scale, so your apparent weight is higher. When it accelerates down, it's like you're lifted, so your apparent weight is less. If the cable snaps, the scale reads zero because you and the scale are both falling at the same rate."

"Cool. So in the kind of free-fall rides that shoot you up, that's why you feel so heavy?" I think I was finally getting it. "Like the up elevator, but way faster, so you get an apparent weight of, like, a million *g*s?" I asked.

Liam interrupted. "What are you talking about, a million *g*s… what's a *g*?"

Stephen Hawking (1942-)
Richard Feynman (1918-1988)

Fun physicists? Like antimatter, they do exist. Stephen Hawking's a fun guy. His work lies in the deep-thinking realm of theoretical astrophysics and cosmology. He discovered in the 1970s that black holes aren't truly black—they leak out subatomic particles that are now called Hawking radiation. Back then, he also bet that once a black hole swallowed something, all its information was gone for good. In 2004, he lost this bet and cheerfully handed over a set of encyclopedias (which always gives up information) to the winner. Hawking's books, including *A Brief History of Time*, are bestsellers, and he's appeared on *The Simpsons* and *Star Trek: The Next Generation*. He dreams of space travel, and in April 2007 the 65-year-old physicist took a first step toward this goal. He left his wheelchair and did flips during eight 25-second microgravity-inducing plunges aboard a Vomit Comet at the Kennedy Space Center.

Richard Feynman worked on the Manhattan Project team, the team that built the first atomic bomb. In his spare time, he liked to pick the locks on filing cabinets full of classified information and leave notes about lax security inside. His popular books carried titles like *Surely You're Joking, Mr. Feynman!* and *What Do You Care What Other People Think?* But seriously, he received a Nobel Prize for his work in quantum electrodynamics, which included a simple way to chart the scattering of colliding particles (Feynman diagrams). Dramatically, he dunked an o-ring into a glass of ice water and showed the world, on live television, that the shrunken rubber didn't bounce back—which was why the *Challenger* space shuttle exploded in midair in 1986. Feynman practically invented nanotechnology, with his big dreams for the world of small.

"A 'g' is a short way to talk about the acceleration caused by gravity. One g is 9.8 meters per second squared, or about 32 feet per second squared—that tells you how fast gravity changes your velocity every second. So a million gs is a huge acceleration," answered Audrey. Then she laughed. "Those slingshot rides aren't giving you quite that much. High-g forces can suck the blood down right out of your brain. Most people black out at 5 gs, fighter pilots can take 9 gs, and the max anyone's survived is 180 gs—that was a Formula One race-car driver who felt that massive g-force for only a fraction of a second."

JEREMY WRESTLES WITH THE WEIRD STUFF...

Gravity is tug of war on a massive scale. Earth pulls on us, we pull on it. Guess who wins that one? Earth also tugs on the moon, and the moon tugs back. But while the moon's strong enough to lift ocean water so we get our daily tides, it's not enough to turn the tables and get Earth circling the moon. Next round: Earth versus sun—and the sun wins! But it's not over. Competition is happening on all fronts because gravity exists between all objects, according to Newton's law of universal gravitation. It says everything in the universe attracts everything else with a force that's strongest up close. And just like tug of war, the bigger mass beats the rest. It's enough to give a guy an inferiority complex...

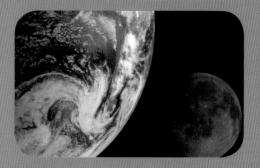

Jaime wanted to ride the roller coaster next, so that's where we headed. As we waited for our turn, Audrey asked us, "What's the best part of the ride for you?"

"The danger—I need speed," Jen said.

the commute to space is a little inconvenient, making your own microgravity makes sense. When NASA needs zero-*g* conditions for research, they fly low-*g* aircraft like the Vomit Comet (aka, the C-9 Low-G Flight Research aircraft) in up-and-down arcs. The sudden dives and steep curves create 20 to 25 seconds of microgravity. Parts of the film *Apollo 13* were filmed in a NASA low-*g* aircraft. No pilot available? Astronauts can opt for one of NASA's drop towers: the Zero Gravity Research Facility's 150-meter (500-foot) shaft gets you 5 seconds of microgravity; its 30-meter (100-foot) Drop Tower gets you 2.2. For an authentic, personal long-term space experience, lie slanted with your head 6 degrees lower than your feet for a couple of days. Or maybe not: your bones, your muscles, and your ability to pump oxygen around will weaken, just like during real space travel.

"For me, it's the hills," added Jaime. "It's so weird—sometimes you feel so heavy and squashed right into your seat, and other times, you're floating!"

"So basically, you like the same apparent weight effects you get from free-fall rides," said Audrey, "and you like acceleration— all that speeding up, slowing down, and changing direction. That's Newton all over again: both his gravitation law and his laws of motion."

"Newton's like the king of rides," Angus said. Angus and Lucas had come running from the bumper cars and were sliding into line in front of us. They filled Jaime and Jen in on bumper-car physics. I could kind of relate...rides are no fun if they don't move, after all.

"The coolest thing about coasters," said Audrey, "is that you feel forces that aren't real. When you accelerate forward, you feel a force pushing you back into your seat—but there can't be a force because there's nothing actually accelerating you in that direction. It's just your inertia, resisting the forward motion."

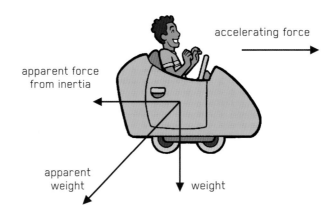

apparent force
from inertia

accelerating force

apparent
weight

weight

"So it's the same for turns, then: when the coaster jolts left on the track, you actually do accelerate left," said Jen. "At the same time, you feel something gluing you to the right, but that's just inertia wanting you to go straight."

"And what about those weird weight changes you get going up and down hills?" asked Jaime.

"Same reason, different direction," replied Audrey. "Real force accelerates you down fast, but you feel like a force is pushing you upward—"

"Which it isn't," supplied Jaime.

Audrey nodded. "So like that elevator example, your apparent weight is less. You feel lighter as you hurtle down the hill. If you accelerate down fast enough, you won't have enough real weight to keep you in your seat without a seatbelt. And if you're going down with just the right acceleration to cancel your weight downward…"

"Then you feel weightless—you're in free fall!" I burst out. An elbow from Liam told me to curb the enthusiasm.

"And that super-heavy feeling?" Jaime asked.

"In a coaster just hitting the bottom of one hill and pulling up the next," said Audrey, "you feel an apparent weight that pulls you against your seat big-time, 3.7 gs on some coasters."

"You can stop talking now. The coaster's emptied out and you kids are up next," said Liam, relieved. "I'll wait by the Pirate Ship." He pointed to where the giant boat hung from its stand.

We got on, me scrambling for the last car, where you could really feel the ups and downs. There was probably a physics lesson in that, too. Better not to say anything, with Audrey sitting beside me!

rider feels light going down the hill

rider feels heavy going through the valley and up the hill

When we finished with the coaster, we found Liam standing with Oscar, a short way from the Pirate Ship. Oscar's head swiveled as he followed the boat's arcing sweep across the sky. "This would look good as a sculpture," he said.

"Sure, Oscar," I said, but I wasn't exactly listening. I was clambering into the boat. The others followed, Liam included. "Hey, are there g-forces on this ride too?" If I could've stuffed the words back into my mouth, I would have. Any other time, being interested would be okay, but the plan was to focus on the fun.

"The g-forces are low as you swing to the top of the arc, and highest when you sweep through the bottom," confirmed Audrey, who was sitting beside me. "If this ride had no motor controlling the speed, it'd be a great example of a pendulum. True pendulums fall only because of gravity, with energy changing from kinetic in the middle—with a small bit of potential, since it hangs off the ground—to all potential at the ends."

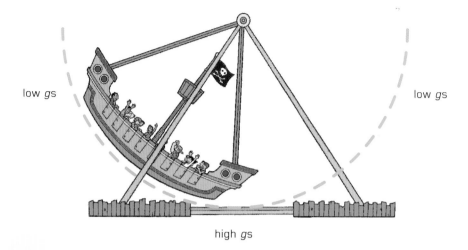

low *gs*

low *gs*

high *gs*

Liam didn't look so good after that ride, either. He staggered after us to the carousel, where we each chose a horse and Liam found a bench. "Looks like this is more your speed," Oscar said to Liam with a smirk. "Just around and around, slow and steady. No acceleration."

"Well...not quite," said Audrey. "Don't forget that acceleration isn't just speeding up; it's also changing direction. When objects travel in a circle, there's always a force pulling them inward. It's called centripetal acceleration—centripetal means center-seeking."

"Inward?" Liam interrupted. "I think you're wrong. I feel like I'm being pushed outward."

"That's not really a force," replied Audrey. "It's your inertia wanting you to keep going ahead, even though the horses are circling. Without the centripetal force, you'd fly off in a straight line."

"What's keeping you from being thrown off, then, if you're standing and don't hold on?" asked Oscar, hopping onto the carousel platform.

"You're probably not going fast enough to beat friction," said Audrey, when he circled back around and jumped off. "Friction keeps you from slipping out of the circle. But just in case, see the

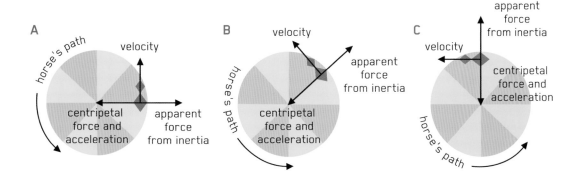

A horse's path — velocity — centripetal force and acceleration — apparent force from inertia

B velocity — apparent force from inertia — horse's path — centripetal force and acceleration

C apparent force from inertia — velocity — centripetal force and acceleration — horse's path

poles and the benches, how they lean inward? That's like banking in a skateboard park. The leaning changes the outward push to a downward one."

After that, it was on to the Wave Swinger. We climbed into the swings and dangled there, waiting for the long chains to toss us up and around in a circle. "Bet this one works the same way," said Oscar.

Audrey nodded. "The force that pulls the riders inward comes from the chains. And in that ride over there, it's the walls."

She was talking about the Barrel of Fun, which, personally, I hated. You stand with your back against the inside of a spinning cylinder while the floor drops to reveal a yawning pit. Fun? I think not.

"The centripetal force from the wall keeps you from spinning out," she continued, "and the friction between you and the wall balances your weight, pulling you down."

From our swings, we saw operators across the grounds cutting off the lineups to the rides. This was it, then. When our ride was over, we headed out with the others. Liam stationed himself at the gate and reminded everyone to fight for their fair at the meeting that followed. No one else said much. Like me, all the kids were busy filing away memories of what might have been their last rides ever.

Liam and I crossed over to the building where the meeting was being held. Inside, we ran smack into what looked like the whole town, waiting in the hall outside a closed door. "They're rearranging the chairs to make room," grumbled one woman. "They weren't expecting quite so many kids." I just smiled at her. Kids count, too, you know. I spied Audrey up ahead, and she waited for us as the doors opened and the crowd moved in.

Would the tide turn for fun, or for physics? I squeezed in between two filing cabinets near the front. The mayor fiddled with the microphone, thanked the crowd for coming, and then got right to the point. "We are here because one of our citizens," he said, looking at Liam, "has raised concerns about our newest construction opportunity." Checking the newspaper on the podium in front of him, he continued, "This person believes that replacing the amusement park with a physics research building will hurt, rather than help, our town. Does anybody share this concern?"

Audrey opened her mouth, but I beat her to it. "The fair and rides are the best part of the whole year—you can't take it away!" At least a dozen kids shouted more or less the same thing. I pulled myself back into the gap between the filing cabinets to escape Audrey's hurt look, while the mayor shouted for silence.

"One at a time, please. Six weeks of fun is no substitute for your futures," began the mayor. He broke off as his cell phone rang. Giving an embarrassed laugh, he shut it off and said, "And a reminder: let's all turn off our cell phones and any other electronic devices during the meeting."

At the word "electronic," Audrey jolted straight up in her seat and said, "You were talking about how the fair lasts only six weeks." She twisted around to face the kids. "Think about it—what would be worse: six weeks without a fair or a lifetime without your computer games, television, CD player, or Nintendo Wii or DS? Those things depend on the physics of electrons." Horrified whispers circulated the room.

"I don't really get why electrons are important here," said Nick from two rows back. "I mean, yeah, it's one of the particles everything's made of. And duh, electrons, electronics—there's got to be a connection. Just what is it?"

"You're right about the connection," said Audrey. "Electricity is the energy that powers electronic devices, and it comes from the movement of charged particles—usually electrons. We call moving charges electric current."

"What makes them move?" asked Nick. "And how does that give you energy?"

"The attraction between opposite charges makes them move," said Audrey. "A negatively charged particle like an electron moves toward anything positively charged. So holding it back stores up energy in the electron, kind of like storing energy in an elastic by stretching it. The more you store up, the more potential energy you've got. Electrical potential energy is measured in volts."

Protons are positive, electrons are negative. You can't keep protons and electrons apart because opposites attract. But protons reject protons every time; same goes when electrons get together. Whether it's attraction or rejection, Coulomb's law says that the force is strongest up close, and it weakens with distance. The rule also says that strength comes in numbers. One lonely charge is harmless, but when they gang up, watch out! Ever scuff your feet across carpet? Every step loads your running shoes with negative charge. Brought close to a doorknob, all that negative charge sends doorknob electrons to the back...leaving protons up front. Mutual attraction starts the sparks flying.

"So to run something like a light bulb or a Gameboy, you need to build one pile of negative charge and another pile of positive charge, and then keep electrons from crossing over to the positive pile until you're ready?" asked Nick.

"Build piles of charge. I see." Liam faced Audrey. "And how does physics expect us to do this—by scooping up particles and sorting them one by one?" That got some laughs from the crowd.

Audrey ignored the jeer in Liam's voice. "Your piles could be two battery terminals, where a chemical reaction heaps negative particles at one terminal and positive ones at the other—that's why batteries are marked plus and minus."

Uh...I'm not always the brightest bulb in the box, but I thought electrons did the moving in a conductor...so how come we draw circuits showing current flow from (+) to (–)? This setup should send electrons screaming the other way! Audrey says that Benjamin Franklin messed up when he chose which to call what, so we just pretend that it's positive charge moving. Don't blame Franklin, though; electrons weren't discovered for another 145 years!

She grabbed a marker and started a sketch on the whiteboard above my head. "So here's how it works. This is a battery, with one end full of positive charge, the other end full of negative. One wire connects the plus terminal to something that needs energy, like a light bulb, and another connects the bulb back to the battery, at its minus terminal. That makes a circuit, and when it's closed, it's a path for electrons from energy source to energy eater and back," said Audrey.

"What do you mean 'when it's closed'?" asked one woman.

"If this path is disconnected at any point, say by an off switch, the circuit is open," replied Audrey. "And the electrons can't move. But as soon as you close it, electrons all along the wire head to the positive pile.

electricity

and magnetism: they have their differences, but like pb and j, they're better together. Electricity's useful around the house, magnets too—and not just for sticking stuff. Magnetic patterns code information on credit cards and computer disks. A really strong magnet can levitate frogs, fruit, anything with molecules that automatically repel an outside magnet. Moving magnets can make electric current flow, and flowing current creates magnets. So cooperation makes sense: you'll find electromagnets in the motors of toy cars, hairdryers, washing machines, and in generators making power. In televisions, magnets guide high-speed electrons as they light dots across the screen. Superconducting magnets can lift and move high-speed trains, too. And together, they create the ultimate, original dynamic duo: the electro-magnetic spectrum.

As each one passes the bulb, it dumps its cargo of energy and moves on, returning to the energy source for more."

"Does this path have to be a wire?" another voice asked.

"It can be any material that has enough electrons that can move," said Audrey. "Most materials can be sorted into conductors, insulators, or semiconductors. When connected in a circuit, good conductors like copper have electrons that can easily pick up enough energy to move from the negative terminal to the positive one. Insulators like glass or plastic can't do this—"

"And a semiconductor would be something in between?" I guessed.

"Exactly," said Audrey. "Like the silicon used in computer chips. A semiconductor's ability to conduct is so-so. The important thing is that it's easy to change by doping it."

"Doping?" said the mayor. "I think you'd better explain that one."

when

a battery dies, you can't really recharge it. But no worries: it's not new charge that's needed. In a dead battery, all the chemicals have reacted and turned into other stuff in the process of separating charges and giving you energy. But the chemical reaction in rechargeable batteries is reversible, so by plugging in the recharger and resupplying energy, you get back what you started with. Rechargeable batteries are legit, just badly named. Call them re-energizables instead.

"Doping is adding small amounts of atoms from other materials to a pure semiconductor," said Audrey. "This ups the semiconductor's ability to conduct, big-time. Doping creates two types of semiconductors, which can be arranged to guide current any way you like through them. It's perfect for making transistors, which are the millions of on/off switches in integrated circuits."

"Those are computer chips, right?" Nick asked.

"That's right," said Audrey. "Now imagine your life without computer chips!"

No MP3, no computer games, no Internet...I'd never survive. And from what I could hear from the buzz in the room around me, no one else could either. Faced with that, nobody was saving that summer fair. But...

"Wait one minute!" cried Liam. "If we were talking about some high-tech factory to churn out transistors or assemble computers and other gadgets, I could see your point. But a research center? We've already got the technology, so why throw money away on useless research?"

"Electricity and transistors may have been around for ages," said Audrey, "but research never stops."

"He makes sense," said one woman. "Research is so theoretical."

"Meaning useless," said Liam.

"Theory is not useless," argued Audrey. "Look at quantum mechanics—it describes the world of atoms and smaller particles, just like Newton's laws explain how the full-sized world works. It's a totally different world: particles are waves, waves are particles, and you never really know fully where tiny particles are or exactly what they're like."

"And how could that possibly be useful to any of us?" Liam spluttered.

"Working with individual atoms, photons, or any nano-sized particles lets you build amazing structures," replied Audrey. "That's what nanotechnology's all about. Some of the stuff discovered recently could make it easy to pack information into individual atoms. Imagine 30,000 movies stored in something the size of an iPod or computers that run so fast on quantum bits—qubits for short—they take only seconds to solve problems that normal computers can't do at all."

"Nanotechnology, eh?" the mayor said. "That's exactly the direction our town should be heading in. I think that settles it. Unless anybody else has serious objections, the town will be supporting the building of the research center."

No one spoke up, so the mayor adjourned the meeting and the crowd rose to go, scraping their chairs. But Liam wasn't ready to

more transistors are produced every year than grains of rice. Roughly 450 billion kilograms (about 990 billion pounds) of rice, about 27×10^{15} grains, were grown worldwide in 2002. So you know how some people say, "If wishes were horses, beggars would ride"? Well, if transistors were rice...*bon appetit!*

Let's see if I've got this straight. At the quantum level, matter is energy, particles and waves are one, and reality is unreal!

Or at least uncertain, until you look at it. And—according to quantum physicists who themselves don't fully understand it all—this is the only way the world makes sense!

give up yet. "Wait!" he called in his booming voice. "Think past the glitz—has it occurred to anybody that we rely far too much on technology and electricity? Sure, research gives us faster and better machines, but what happens to us? It makes us pampered, lazy, and useless."

He paused, looking around at the crowd. "That's not for me. I'm not feeding into any self-defeating research. All *I* need to survive—no, thrive—is this," he said, tapping the side of his head. "Not physics in any shape or form."

TAP TAP

"That might be harder than you think," said Audrey, "since your brain runs on electricity."

"What kind of Frankenstein scenario are you suggesting?" Liam was almost shouting by this point. "Do you see wires sprouting from my ears?"

"Your brain holds about a hundred billion nerve cells, and each one connects thousands of others into a powerful electrical network that's so complex it beats the Internet, hands down," responded Audrey. "At each thought, nerve cells—they're called neurons—fire off a signal that shifts positive electric charge down to its end.

There, a chemical ferries the message across the gap to the next nerve, where the message turns electrical again and speeds away, from neuron to neuron until it reaches its destination."

Liam opened his mouth to argue, but nothing came out. A disconnect between brain and voice box? Or maybe a light bulb finally lit up somewhere in his mind. Whatever the reason, the end result of the electricity blipping through his brain got his mouth shut and his feet moving, right out the door.

Plans are now afoot for a shiny, state-of-the-art physics research center. Construction's not starting for another six weeks, though, because guess what? Audrey hinted to the university that the amusement-park rides were a great learning experience, and the university suddenly came up with this amendment to their plans: let's keep the rides on the grounds and make them a part of our public-outreach program. How brilliant was that?

The XIV Symposium on the Universality of Physics went ahead on schedule and as planned—but not, whew, the classes. Instead, Valerie Ryan coaxed some other physicists into setting up a section of the conference for kids and non-scientists, and the topics and work-shops were awesome!

One physicist gained some groupies—Angus, Lucas, Nick, and a few of Nick's boarder buddies—after a demo on the physics of skate-boards. They finally left her alone after she promised to come back in the winter to talk about snowboards. After that, the guys moved on to spend major time in front of a model of the Large Hadron Collider. Having mastered collisions on the macroscopic level, they obviously wanted some smash-em-up on the subatomic scale.

Another professor talked us through our favorite comic books and sci-fi fantasy novels, pointing out where the writers had it right, and where they went wrong, physics-wise. Oscar had some questions about cartoon physics—how come gravity only kicks in when the characters clue in, for instance—and, well, let's just say *that* session ran overtime. If I know Oscar, after the conference he'll be checking over all the cartoon art back at the gallery and telling visitors how the physics went funny.

Jen and Jaime were late for Valerie Ryan's talk, but managed to catch most of it. She showed magnetic resonance imaging (MRI) scans of her brain, pictures built using magnets and radio waves, to show which parts of her brain were busiest when she improvised or played scales. Of course, she wound up her session with a few songs. That got Jen and Jaime talking about some research they'd heard about in the morning. Some physicists were working on something called rough silicon nanowires to capture and convert waste heat—from your body, a car, or regular power plants, for example—into electricity. The girls couldn't wait for the day when they'd be listening to Valerie's songs on iPods charged by their very own personal power jackets. Never mind iPods: think what it means for the world energy supply!

I almost skipped this one, a science film called *Physics Based Simulations for Realistic Flow*. But talk about blowing your low expectations: for an hour, we witnessed the biggest, baddest explosions ever, splattered across a Jumbotron screen. Turns out a lot of physicists work in animation, building physics-based programs to create believable water, clouds, smoke, and explosions for movies and video games.

Once in a while, Audrey and I would stray from the kids' section and stumble into a room full of physicists. We'd sit and listen, letting phrases like "superfluid properties of Bose–Einstein condensed atoms," "fluctuation-dissipation theorem," "quantum chromodynamics," and "biphotonic qutrits" just wash over us. It was cool when I understood bits—not that it happened often.

Doesn't matter. Mission accomplished, and then some.

Glossary

Absolute zero: Zero degrees Kelvin, equal to –273.15 degrees Celsius or –459.67 degrees Fahrenheit, the lowest possible temperature.

Acceleration: How fast an object's velocity is changing (speeding up, slowing down, or turning) over time.

Acoustics: The science of sound.

Aerodynamics: The science describing how air or any other gas flows and affects solid things moving through it.

Altitude: The height of anything above a certain point, such as sea level.

Amplitude: The property of a wave that indicates wave strength by measuring how much it changes or disturbs the medium it crosses.

Antimatter: The exact equal but opposite of matter; for example, an anti-electron is a positron, which behaves exactly like an electron with a positive (instead of negative) charge. Matter and antimatter are created together from energy.

Astronomy: The scientific study of space, its galaxies, stars, and planets; astronomy includes both astrophysics and cosmology.

Astrophysics: The science that describes and measures the composition and characteristics of stars and other celestial objects.

Atmospheric thermodynamics: The science of heat and energy movement in the earth's atmosphere; the physics of clouds and precipitation.

Atom: A tiny particle made of a nucleus surrounded by one or more electrons; the smallest recognizable part of any element.

Beat: The regularly repeating changes in sound intensity that come from two almost identical waves interfering with each other as they travel the same space.

Big Bang: An ultra-hot expansion about 14 billion years ago that most astrophysicists believe resulted in our universe.

Biphotonic qutrit: In quantum computing, information stored in two photons following quantum rules that allow far-faster data processing than regular computers can accomplish.

Black hole: A region of space created by the collapse of massive stars, where a huge amount of mass is compacted into a tiny volume and gravity is so strong that nothing entering the black hole can escape.

Bose-Einstein condensate: An ultra-dense state of matter formed at temperatures near absolute zero (one of five basic forms of matter).

Boundary layer: The layer of air or gas molecules closest to an object moving through the air or the gas.

Brane: An object in string and M-theory; for example, a one-brane is a string, a two-brane is a membrane.

Calculus: The name for two types of mathematics. Integral calculus is one way of computing areas and volumes of complicated shapes. Differential calculus computes constantly changing values, such as how fast you're traveling on a trip where the car's speed keeps changing.

Centripetal acceleration: Acceleration directed inward for an object traveling in a circle.

Circuit: A path electrons follow from energy source through energy eaters and back.

Compression: In a sound wave, a zone where the air molecules are squashed together.

Condensation: The change from a gas to a liquid state.

Conduction: The process in which thermal energy passes from molecule to molecule, by direct contact.

Conductor: A material with electrons that can easily pick up enough energy to move from the negative terminal to the positive one.

Conservation of momentum: A universal physics law that says there must be the same total amount of momentum before and after a collision.

Convection: The process in which thermal energy moves within a fluid (liquid or gas).

Coriolis effect: The influence of the earth's rotation (fastest at the equator, slowest near the poles) on the direction of an object or a fluid, pushing toward the right in the northern hemisphere and the left in the southern hemisphere. Commonly used to explain wind movement.

Cosmology: The scientific study of the origin and evolution of the universe.

Coulomb's law: A rule that describes the force between two charged particles. It says that the force weakens with distance and depends on how strongly charged the particles are.

Curie: A unit for radiation level.

Dark energy: The mysterious form of energy found in the vacuum of space, thought to be causing the accelerating expansion of the universe.

Dark matter: Matter that can't be seen because it doesn't emit or reflect light.

Density: A ratio that compares an object's mass to its volume.

Doping: Adding small amounts of atoms from other materials to a pure semiconductor to make it a better conductor.

Drag: The overall slowing force that results when pressure in front of a moving object is greater than the pressure behind it.

Electric current: Charges moving in response to an electric field (attraction between opposite charges). Current is measured as how fast charge flows past a specific point in a circuit, in amperes.

Electrical potential energy: The energy stored up when positive and negative charges are separated, measured as electrical potential difference, in volts.

Electromagnet: A temporary magnet created when a current passes through a wire wrapped around an iron core.

Electromagnetic force: One of four known fundamental forces; this force is carried by photons and is seen in the interaction between charges and in magnets.

Electromagnetic radiation (EMR): Any wavelength of visible or invisible light; a pair of electric and magnetic fields occurring together, at right angles.

Electromagnetic spectrum: The entire range of visible and invisible light waves arranged according to their wavelengths.

Electron: A subatomic particle with a charge of −1.

Element: The simplest type of matter, made up of only one type of atom, such as hydrogen or gold.

Energy: The capacity to do work or make things happen.

Evaporation: The change from a liquid to a gas state.

Feynman diagram: A simple way to chart the scattering of colliding particles.

First Law of Thermodynamics: The total energy in the universe is conserved, and the only way that any stationary object in the universe can change its own energy is by doing work or transferring heat.

Fluctuation–dissipation theorem: An idea used in statistical physics to make predictions based on what happens in systems where temperatures have stopped changing.

Force: A push or pull that results in the acceleration of a mass. Four fundamental forces are known to exist: gravity, electromagnetic force, weak force, and strong force.

Free fall: Falling under the influence of gravity alone.

Frequency: How many waves pass by a point each second, measured in hertz (cycles per second).

Friction: The force that opposes motion between two touching surfaces.

g: A short way to talk about the acceleration caused by gravity. One *g* is 9.8 meters per second squared, or about 32 feet per second squared.

Galaxy: A collection of stars, gas, and dust held together by gravity.

Gas: A state of matter in which the molecules are spread out and attractive forces are weak, so it has no fixed shape or volume (one of five basic forms of matter).

General Theory of Relativity: Einstein's theory of gravitation, which says that gravity is the effect caused by the bending of space-time by objects in the universe.

Gluon: The particle that carries the strong force.

Gravity: The weakest of the four known fundamental forces.

Harmonics: A set of standing waves in which the frequencies are whole number ratios of the lowest frequency.

Hawking radiation: The tiny amount of radiation emitted from a black hole, predicted by physicist Stephen Hawking.

Heat: A process for transferring energy, driven by differences in temperature.

Heisenberg's Uncertainty Principle: The position and momentum of a quantum object, such as a particle, are impossible to measure accurately at the same time because observing the particle changes it.

Hertz (Hz): The unit for measuring frequency (cycles per second).

Humidity: The percentage of water in air.

Inertia: The characteristic that causes something with mass to stay resting if it's resting, or to keep going at a steady pace in the same direction until some force changes it.

Infrasonic: Describes frequencies lower than the normal range heard by human ears, below about 20 hertz.

Insulator: A material with electrons that cannot easily pick up enough energy to move from the negative terminal to the positive one.

Integrated circuit: Also called a computer chip, a tiny circuit etched on a piece of silicon.

Intensity: How powerfully sound energy pounds your eardrum, measured in decibels.

Interference: When waves run into each other and merge into a new wave pattern.

Kinetic energy: Energy in action.

Law of Conservation of Energy: A universal rule that says the total amount of energy in the universe never changes, but can shift through different forms.

Lepton: A fundamental particle; the electron, muon, tau, and three types of neutrinos are leptons.

Lift: A force created by an object moving through a fluid. Lift forces keep an airplane up as it flies through the air, but can also push a ball sideways or down.

Light-speed: How fast light travels in a vacuum, abbreviated as c and exactly equal to 299,792,458 meters per second (over 1 billion kilometers an hour, or 0.7 billion miles an hour).

Liquid: A state of matter that has little space between particles and can change shape, but not volume (one of five basic forms of matter).

Longitudinal wave: A wave in which both the disturbance and the wave go in the same direction.

Magnetic resonance imaging (MRI) scan: Pictures built using magnets and radio waves.

Magnetism: A force created by spinning electrons within a material and resulting in the attraction of other materials such as iron or the repulsion of materials such as water.

Many-worlds theory: A theory that says every possible result from every choice exists as a separate universe.

Mass: The total amount of matter that makes something.

Matrix mechanics: The theory using mathematical objects called matrices that Werner Heisenberg used to calculate a particle's motion, based on light emitted and absorbed by atoms.

Matter: Everything you see in the universe. There are five basic forms of matter: solid, liquid, gas, plasma, and Bose-Einstein condensate. *See also* Dark matter; State (of matter).

Microgravity: Zero-*g* conditions, resulting in apparent weightlessness.

Molecule: Atoms joined in certain combinations.

Momentum: A measure of motion based on the mass and speed of a moving object. Objects moving in a straight line have linear momentum, while turning or spinning objects have angular momentum.

M-theory: A theory that says our universe is a separate 11-dimensional membrane (a brane) that shares gravity with other branes carrying other universes.

Muon: A lepton with the same charge but more mass than an electron.

Nanotechnology: The study of matter on the scale of nanometers (one nanometer is a millionth of a millimeter or 40 billionths of an inch in size) in order to make useful technologies.

Neuron: Nerve cell.

Newton's First Law of Motion: An object stays at rest if originally resting or it keeps going at the same speed and direction if already moving, until another force changes its motion.

Newton's Law of Universal Gravitation: Everything in the universe attracts everything else with a force that is strongest up close and between more massive objects.

Newton's Laws of Motion: Sir Isaac Newton's explanation for the behavior of everything moving in the ordinary world.

Newton's Second Law of Motion: Force = mass x acceleration. The equation says that an object accelerates faster when a greater force is applied, or when a less massive object is used.

Newton's Third Law of Motion: If one thing pushes on another, the second thing pushes back with equal force.

Nobel Prize: An honored worldwide prize given for discoveries in physics, chemistry, medicine, literature, and peace.

Nuclear fusion: A process that releases energy with the combination of atomic nuclei to form new, heavier nuclei.

Nuclei: The plural of nucleus. *See* Atom.

Particle: A tiny bit of matter.

Pendulum: A suspended body that swings back and forth in a regular pattern.

Photon: A particle of light; the carrier particle for electromagnetic force.

Physics: The science of matter, energy, space, time, and the relations between them.

Plasma: This state of matter is a gas of ionized atoms (one of five basic forms of matter).

Plasmon: An electron wave, formed by a regularly repeating pattern of electrons passing in bunches.

Potential energy: Stored energy.

Pulsar: A collapsed star that emits regular signals as it rotates.

Quantum chromodynamics: The theory explaining quark and gluon interaction.

Quantum entanglement: A way particles can jumble together so that changing one instantly changes the other.

Quantum mechanics: The rules describing the behavior of atoms and smaller particles.

Quark: A fundamental particle making up protons and neutrons. Quarks exist in six varieties (up, down, charm, strange, top, bottom) and three "colors" (red, green, blue) and are held together by gluons of strong force.

Qubit (quantum bit): In quantum computing, information stored in a photon or other particle following quantum rules that allow far-faster data processing than regular computers can accomplish.

Radiation: Heat moving across space as electromagnetic waves.

Radioactive: The term used to describe atoms whose nuclei eject particles and energy through a very slow, really random process called tunneling.

Rarefaction: In a sound wave, a zone where the air molecules are far apart.

Reflection: When light bounces off a surface.

Refraction: The bending of light as it passes from one material into another.

Refractive index: A number comparing the speed of light in a vacuum and the speed of light in a particular material.

Resonance: Occurs when the vibration from one object matches the natural frequency of another and sets the second object vibrating.

Schrödinger's cat paradox: An imaginary experiment involving radioactive atoms and a cat that is alive and dead at the same time.

Schrödinger's wave equation: An equation describing the wavelike behavior of particles.

Second Law of Thermodynamics: An event occurs only if doing so lowers the overall energy state.

Semiconductor: A material whose ability to conduct is easily controlled.

SETI (Search for Extraterrestrial Intelligence): An effort to detect alien civilizations possessing technologies equal to or more advanced than our own. The SETI Institute is a non-profit group committed to research and projects that study life in the universe.

Solid: This state of matter has closely packed particles and cannot change volume or shape (one of five basic forms of matter).

Special Theory of Relativity: Einstein's theory that says everybody sees light moving at the same speed and uses the same laws of physics whether they're moving steadily or standing still.

Spectroscopy: A technique for measuring how a sample absorbs or sends back different kinds of light.

Standard Model of the Atom: The currently accepted theory describing all matter as based on quarks, leptons, and forces that act through carrier particles. Gluons of strong force glue quarks together to form protons and neutrons, and bind protons and neutrons into atomic nuclei. Photons of electromagnetic force join electrons to these nuclei. Through W and Z bosons, the weak force causes radioactive decay of heavy particles into smaller ones. The Standard Model is considered incomplete until gravity can be explained at atomic scale and the Higgs boson, a particle giving all other particles mass, is found.

Standing wave pattern: The pattern that results when a wave reflects back on itself.

State (of matter): One of five basic forms of matter: solid, liquid, gas, plasma, and Bose-Einstein condensate.

Strong force: One of four known fundamental forces; the nuclear force that keeps quarks, protons, and neutrons together in an atom and is carried by gluons.

Superfluid: A liquid or gas with no viscosity.

Supernova: The explosive death of a massive star, occurring after the star uses up its nuclear fuel.

Superstring theory: A theory of the universe in which it has six more hidden dimensions, and each particle type is a string or a loop plucked to vibrate in its own special way.

Teleportation: The transfer of an object by causing it to disappear from one place and instantly reappear in another.

Thermoacoustic: A term used to describe a method of cooling with sound.

Thermodynamics: The science that studies how energy moves, through work and heat.

Third Law of Thermodynamics: At absolute zero (–273°C/–460°F) in a perfect crystal, no molecules move.

Transistor: An electrical device that switches on or off to let current through an integrated circuit.

Transpire: To evaporate from plants.

Transverse wave: A wave in which the disturbance travels at right angles to the direction of the wave.

Turbulence: A roughness in the flow of a gas, such as air.

Ultrasonic: Describes frequencies higher than the normal range of hearing, over 20,000 hertz.

Universe: Everything that exists, including dark matter and dark energy.

Velocity: A measure of how fast something's position changes over time.

Viscosity: Friction between layers of fluid (or stickiness between fluid molecules).

Visible light: Radiation in the visible part of the electromagnetic spectrum.

W and Z bosons: Particles that carry weak force.

Wake: A low-pressure area following a moving object.

Wavelength: The distance between pattern repeats (from crest to crest or trough to trough) in a wave.

Weak force: One of four known fundamental forces; this force is responsible for interactions involving radioactivity and is carried by W and Z bosons.

Weight: A force; how strongly gravity pulls you to the center of the earth.

Work: A process for transferring energy. Work is done only when you move something over a distance.

Wormhole: A tunnel-like structure connecting two separate locations in space-time. Traveling through a wormhole could in theory take much less time than traveling through normal space. The math in general relativity allows wormholes to exist but, so far, physicists have no proof.

Zeroth Law of Thermodynamics: If two things are each at the same temperature as a third, then the two must also be at the same temperature.

Further Reading

Gribbin, Mary and John. *The Science of Philip Pullman's "His Dark Materials"* (Laurel Leaf, 2007).

Hawking, Lucy and Stephen. *George's Secret Key to the Universe* (Simon and Schuster, 2007).

Krull, Kathleen. *Isaac Newton (Giants of Science Series)*, illustrated by Boris Kulikov (Viking Penguin, 2006).

MacLeod, Elizabeth. *Albert Einstein: A Life of Genius* (Kids Can Press, 2003).

MacLeod, Elizabeth. *Marie Curie: A Brilliant Life* (Kids Can Press, 2004).

Wiese, Jim. Sports Science: *40 Goal-Scoring, High-Flying, Medal-Winning Experiments for Kids*, illustrated by Ed Shems (John Wiley & Sons, 2002).

For Older Readers

Bodanis, David. *Electric Universe* (Crown, 2006).

Bodanis, David. *E=mc^2* (Walker & Co., 2005).

Feynman, Richard P. *Six Easy Pieces: Essentials of Physics, Explained by Its Most Brilliant Teacher* (Perseus Books, 2005).

Kakalios, James. *The Physics of Superheroes* (Gotham Books, 2005).

Kaku, Michio. *Physics of the Impossible: A Scientific Exploration into the World of Phasers, Force Fields, Teleportation and Time Travel* (Doubleday, 2008).

Krauss, Lawrence. *Fear of Physics: A Guide for the Perplexed* (Perseus Books , 2007).

Newton, Roger. *From Clockwork to Crapshoot: A History of Physics* (Belknap Press, 2006).

Suplee, Curt. *The New Everyday Science Explained: From the Big Bang to the Human Genome...and Everything In Between* (National Geographic Society, 2004).

Interesting Online Resources

"Astronomy Picture of the Day," NASA's picture of the day, appearing with a short explanation by an astronomer, available at http://antwrp.gsfc.nasa.gov/apod/astropix.html

"Educational Outreach–Nobel Prize in Physics," the Nobel Foundation's outreach program, which includes games and productions about Nobel prize-winning technology and research, available at http://nobelprize.org/educational_games/physics/

"Einstein's Big Idea," all about Albert Einstein and his ideas, available at http://www.pbs.org/wgbh/nova/einstein/. "The Power of Small Things," "The Light Stuff," and "Time Traveler" pack some of the biggest ideas into easy-to-understand, interactive capsules.

"Jetstream–Online School for Weather," weather information from the U.S. National Weather Service, available at http://www.srh.weather.gov/jetstream/matrix.htm

"Origins," a NASA site featuring a timeline of the universe, available at http://origins.jpl.nasa.gov/library/poster/poster.html

"The Particle Adventure: The Fundamentals of Matter and Force," an interactive tour of the subatomic world and how these parts make the whole universe, by the Particle Data Group at Lawrence Berkeley National Laboratory, available at http://particleadventure.org

"Physics 2000," a survey of modern physics topics for students by the University of Colorado at Boulder, available at http://www.colorado.edu/physics/2000/index.pl

"Sport Science," a look at the science of various sports by the Exploratorium, a San Francisco museum and education center, available at http://www.exploratorium.edu/sports/

"The Universe Forum," created by the Smithsonian Astrophysical Observatory for NASA, available at http://www.cfa.harvard.edu/seuforum/

Index

absolute zero, 54, 92

acceleration, 27, 69–70, 74, 75, 76, 78, 79, 92

    centripetal acceleration, 78–79, 94

acoustics, 39, 48, 92

aerodynamics, 10–14, 18, 20, 92

amplitude, 28, 92

amusement park rides, physics of:

    bumper cars, 68–70

    carousel, 78–79

    free-fall rides, 71–72, 74

    pendulum rides, 76–78

    roller coaster, 74–77

animation, physics of, 90

antimatter, 62–63, 73, 92

astronomy, 63, 67, 92

astrophysics, 63, 73, 92

atom, 2, 9, 15, 24, 26, 27, 52, 59–64, 86–87, 93

baseball, physics of, 10–18

batteries, 83–84, 86

Becquerel, Henri, 49

Big Bang, 60, 93

black holes, 47, 64–65, 93

Bose–Einstein condensate, 9, 91, 93

boundary layer, 10–13, 93

brane, 65, 93

cartoons, physics of, 90

circuits:

    electric, 84–85

    integrated, 86, 98

collisions, 15, 21, 62, 70, 90

condensation, 57–58, 94

conduction, 55, 94

conductors, 84–85, 94

convection, 55, 94

Coriolis effect, 56, 94

cosmology, 63, 67, 73, 94

Coulomb's Law, 83, 94

Curie, Marie, 49

cycling, physics of, 18

dark energy, 64, 95

dark matter, 64, 95

decibel. *See* intensity

Dirac, Paul Adrien Maurice, 61

distance, 15, 17, 22, 28, 52, 83

doping, 85–86, 95

drag, 10–11, 17, 95

Einstein, Albert, 27, 65

electricity, 82, 85–86, 88–90

    electric current, 82, 85, 95

electromagnet, 62, 85, 95

electromagnetic radiation (EMR), 26, 32, 95

    gamma, 26

    infrared, 26

    microwave, 26

    radio, 3, 26, 90

    ultraviolet, 26

    visible, 26, 30, 32–33

    x-ray, 26, 47, 49

electromagnetic spectrum, 24–26, 96

electron, 9, 59-61, 63, 82-85, 96

element, 9, 41, 49, 63, 96

energy, 2, 16, 18, 21, 26-27, 29, 39, 42, 46-47, 51-56, 60, 62, 77, 82, 84-86, 88, 90, 96

    conservation of, 52-54

    electrical potential, 82, 95

    kinetic, 53-54

    potential, 53, 77, 82, 101

evaporation, 58-59, 96

Feynman, Richard, 73

Feynman diagram, 73, 96

force, 2, 12-13, 19-20, 60, 62, 69-71, 74-79, 83, 96

    electromagnetic, 60, 95

    of gravity, 16, 19, 27, 63, 65, 71-72, 74-75, 77, 90, 97

    and lift, 12-13, 98

    strong, 60, 103

    weak, 60, 105

Franklin, Benjamin, 84

free fall. *See* microgravity

frequency, 28, 42, 46, 96

    infrasonic, 42, 98

    ultrasonic, 42, 104

friction, 20, 54, 56, 69-70, 78-79, 96

g, 72, 74-78, 97

galaxy, 97

gases, 9-13, 18, 48-49, 55, 57, 59, 63, 97

    air, 10-13, 16-18, 29, 31, 41-42, 46, 51, 56-58

    hydrogen, 9, 63

    nitrogen, 10, 18

    oxygen, 9-10, 18, 75

global warming, 58

gluon, 4, 60, 97

gravity, 16, 19, 27, 63, 65, 71-75, 77, 90, 97

harmonics, 45, 97

Hawking, Stephen, 73

Hawking radiation, 97

hearing, physics of, 41-42

heat, 18, 26, 47-48, 52, 54-56, 90, 97

Heisenberg, Werner Karl, 61

hertz (Hz), 42, 97

hockey, physics of, 20-22

humidity, 18, 97

inertia, 69, 72, 75-76, 78-79, 98

instruments, physics of, 38-39, 43-46

insulators, 85, 98

intensity, 46, 98

interference, 3, 43-44, 98

invisibility cloak, 33

Large Hadron Collider (LHC), 62, 90

lepton, 59-60, 98

light. *See* electromagnetic radiation

liquids, 9, 20, 54-55, 99

magnetic resonance imaging (MRI), 90, 99

magnetism, 26, 62, 85, 90, 99

many-worlds theory, 65, 99

mass, 15, 27, 29, 62, 65, 69-71, 74, 99

mass-energy equivalence, 27

matter, 9, 15, 24, 27, 62–64, 88, 99

microgravity, 73, 75, 99

molecule, 9–10, 18, 20, 26, 41–42, 46, 54–56, 85, 99

momentum, 15, 21, 70, 99
    angular, 21, 99
    conservation of, 15, 70, 94
    linear, 15, 99

M-theory, 65, 100

muon, 4, 60, 100

music, physics of, 38–39, 42–45

nanotechnology, 73, 87, 100

NASA, 47, 75

neuron, 88–89, 100

neutrino, 60

Newton, Sir Isaac, laws of, 19, 68–70, 74–75, 87, 100

Nobel Prize, 27, 29, 49, 61, 73, 100

nuclear fusion, 51, 63, 100

nucleus, 26, 59–60, 63, 101

particle accelerator, 62, 90

particles, 9, 24, 27, 29–30, 41, 51, 55, 57, 59–62, 64–65, 73, 82–83, 87–88, 101
    force carrier, 60
    subatomic, 62, 73, 90

photon, 29, 32, 51, 60, 87, 91, 101

plasma, 9, 101

plasmon technology, 33

Pollock, Jackson, 33–34

polonium, 49

pressure, 11, 18, 41, 56, 59

pulsar, 3, 101

quantum entanglement, 24, 101

quantum physics, 24, 27, 29, 61, 73, 87–88, 91

quark, 4, 59–60, 63, 67, 101

qubit (quantum bit), 4, 87, 102

radiation, of heat, 55, 102

radium, 49

reflection, 30–32, 58, 64, 102

refraction, 30–31, 102
    refractive index, 31, 102

relativity, theories of, 27, 61, 65

resonance, 46, 102

Schrödinger, Erwin, 61

semiconductors, 85–86, 102

SETI (Search for Extraterrestrial Intelligence), 3, 103

sight, physics of, 30–32

silicon, 85

solids, 9, 10, 20, 55, 103

sound, physics of, 39–48, 51, 67

spectroscopy, 34–35, 37, 103

Standard Model, of the atom, 60, 103

star, 2, 3, 58–60, 63–65

state (of matter), 9, 27, 103

superfluid, 91, 104

supernova, 63–64, 104

superstring theory, 65–104

tau, 60

teleportation, 24, 104

temperature, 9, 18, 41, 52, 54

thermodynamics: laws of, 54–55, 67,
    96, 102, 104
transistor, 86–87, 104
transpiration, 58
tunneling, 60
turbulence, 11, 18, 104

universe, 4, 9, 19, 26–27, 32, 53–54,
    59–60, 62–65, 74, 104
    expanding universe, 60, 64–65

velocity, 69–70, 74, 105
    of light, 27, 31, 61–62
    of sound, 41, 51
vibrations, 16, 41–43, 46, 48, 65
viscosity, 10, 105
volts, 82
Vomit Comet, 73, 75

wake, 10, 11, 13, 18, 105
W and Z bosons, 60, 105
waves, 26, 28–33, 39–46, 48, 51, 55,
    61, 67, 87–90
    amplitude of, 28, 92
    frequency of, 28, 42, 46, 96
    longitudinal, 39–41, 99
    standing wave pattern, 44–45, 103
    transverse, 28, 40, 104
    wavelength of, 26, 28, 32–33, 105
weather, physics of 54–59
weight, 16, 21, 71–72, 76, 79, 105
    apparent weight, 71, 72, 75–76
work, 52, 54, 105

Photo Credits

Unless otherwise noted, all technical diagrams by 10four design group.

11, 13, 28, 41: © istockphoto.com; 32: © istockphoto.com / René Mansi; 46: © istockphoto.com / Nick Schlax; 54: © istockphoto.com / Michael Valdez; 55: © istockphoto.com / Dean Turner; 63: © istockphoto.com / Rob Sylvan; 85: © istockphoto.com / Jill Fromer

12: © Paul Hakimata / Dreamstime.com; 16: © Todd Taulman / Dreamstime.com; 18: © Valeria Cantone / Dreamstime.com

33: © Dr. Christopher C. Davis, used with permission

40: © Matt Heximer, used with permission

47: courtesy of CXC/NGST

56, 75: courtesy of NASA; 74: courtesy of NASA, JPL

62: © CERN, used with permission

About the Author and Illustrator

Cora Lee is a scientific writer for the biotechnology and pharmaceutical industries. She is the author of *The Great Number Rumble: A Story of Math in Surprising Places* (co-authored by Gillian O'Reilly), and many science articles for kids. Cora lives in Vancouver, BC, where she also volunteers as coordinator for the Vancouver chapter of the Canadian Association for Girls in Science (CAGIS).

Steve Rolston was trained in classical animation and has drawn a wide variety of comics. Most recently, he illustrated the teen graphic novel *Emiko Superstar*, written by Mariko Tamaki. Steve lives in Vancouver, BC.

The Great Number Rumble

by Gillian O'Reilly and Cora Lee

illustrated by Virginia Gray

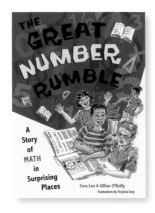

· Science in Society Book Award finalist
· Best Books for Kids & Teens 2008,
  Canadian Children's Book Centre

A plan to nix arithmetic + a math-crazy kid = an entertaining exposé on the wonder of numbers.

When the schools in Jeremy's town ban math, there are loud cheers from the kids. Even his teachers happily toss their textbooks. But Jeremy's best friend Sam, a self-proclaimed math-nik, sets out to prove that math is not only important, but fun.

In the chapters that follow, Sam reveals math's presence in everyday places, including sports (types of triangles determine how a bike functions), art (artist M.C. Escher combined math patterns with imagination), even in nature (ants instinctively calculate dead reckoning—a navigation tool also used by astronauts).

Meanwhile, surprising sidebars offer Jeremy's thoughts on weird concepts from chaos theory to cash prizes for new prime numbers. In the end, Jeremy, his teachers, and even the Director of Education have to admit that school minus math equals all sorts of trouble.

Complete with dozens of amusing real-life math examples, brief bios of seven famous mathematicians, and fun illustrations and diagrams, this innovative introduction to all things arithmetic will win over even the most math-phobic readers.

"Classroom teachers could use this book to introduce new concepts and relate them to everyday objects to help students understand their significance..."
—*School Library Journal*

"...a useful resource to help make math an exciting experience... "
—*Quill & Quire*

"...makes math both relevant and fun."
—*Professionally Speaking: The Magazine of the Ontario College of Teachers*